MONOGRAPH 48

THE AMERICAN ETHNOLOGICAL SOCIETY

Robert F. Spencer, Editor

Black Carib

Household Structure

A STUDY OF MIGRATION AND MODERNIZATION

NANCIE L. SOLIEN GONZALEZ

UNIVERSITY OF WASHINGTON PRESS

SEATTLE AND LONDON

970.3
B627g

87-3185

Originally published by the University of Washington Press as Monograph 48 of the American Ethnological Society

FOR MY MOTHER

FOREWORD

MY enthusiasm for *Black Carib Household Structure* has been maintained over the period of more than ten years that has elapsed since I read it in first draft. The ideas are important, the original field data valuable, and the comparative materials of great utility. The book took its original form as a doctoral dissertation in 1958 and should have been published at once. A series of misfortunes for which Dr. Gonzalez is not responsible has delayed publication. Meantime the value of the book is to be seen in the fact that Dr. Gonzalez' thesis abstract has been repeatedly quoted in the literature on the Caribbean family. The dissertation manuscript, however, has not been so widely used, available, as it is, only in the University Microfilm series. I am exceedingly eager to see the book in print in this new version, in part because I am tired of ordering the microfilm of the original dissertation and asking students to read it in that form. I find that whenever my students plan research on family form and economy, I want them to read the dissertation. Now they can read the book.

The core value of the work is its naturalistic approach to various household forms often described as "broken" or "disorganized": its treatment of these forms as adaptations to specific features of the modern economic scene. In this it departs sharply from a "social problems" view. I think that if I had been writing it, I might have taken the position that there *is* a "social problem" involved: not household form, but the exploitation of the Black Caribs and of others in their situation. Dr. Gonzalez, however, has clearly described this exploitation, even if she has not labeled it.

The delineation of the consanguineal household is another major contribution of *Black Carib Household Structure*. Such a household is a unit containing two or more adults, none of whom is linked to another by affinal bonds. Many "matrifocal" families — if they include two adult sisters without husbands resident in the household, or a mother and adult daughter, both without coresident husbands — fit this definition; other "matrifocal" households — those consisting of a woman with no coresident husband and her immature children — do not. The author's work forces us to pay closer attention to household composition than is ordinarily given to "broken" families. The sharp differentiation of family and household is another important point. These concepts are employed in an analysis of the Black Carib situation, which is then extended comparatively, to relate the existence of the consanguineal household to what the author calls "recurrent" labor migration, which she differentiates from other migration patterns. Dr. Gonzalez also brings out the importance of the compound, as well as the household, for economic adjustment.

This last point is perhaps worth elaboration. Much of the literature on peasant families describes them as nuclear families but does not provide the critical information to enable us to decide whether they are isolated nuclear families minimally interdependent with related families, or nuclear families and households aggregated into highly interdependent compounds or localized clusters. In a few cases there is information — just enough to make it clear that probably all three forms occur. We would expect this type of variation to be related to economic factors, but until it is described, the relationships cannot be discovered. As with the consanguineal household, it is to be hoped that Dr. Gonzalez' stress on the compound will sensitize other field workers.

In this work Dr. Gonzalez develops the concept of a neoteric society, which she regards as a subgroup of a larger, modern society, which retains some cultural diacriticals but lacks "structural self-sufficiency." This concept not only proves useful for the explanation of certain family forms, but is a convenient label for a large number of groups in the modern world. It has been so used by a number of anthropologists who have based themselves on her work.

Finally, of course, there is a harvest of information about the specifics of Black Carib history and culture.

Among the causes of delay in publication have been efforts to keep the manuscript current by references to new research on the Caribbean family. It seems far more important that this manuscript should be published so that other people may refer to it, than that it should be revised so as to refer to other people's work. Its value is considerable and has not lessened with the passage of time.

DAVID F. ABERLE
University of British Columbia

~~~~~~~~~~~~

PREFACE

~~~~~~~~~~~~

THIS monograph is the direct descendant of my doctoral dissertation, started in September, 1957, and completed in July, 1958 (Solien 1959a). Since that time there has been a continuous and apparently increasing scientific interest in the effects of modernization and industrialization upon traditional societies. This is, I suppose, a natural outgrowth of the times. The industrial system seems impelled by its very nature to expand ever outward, gradually drawing within its orbit those societies which even today, at first glance, may appear to be relatively untouched by the age of machines and fossil fuels. Indeed, it is still possible to find many villages and even regions across the face of the earth where the factory system is unknown, and where the labor of producing food and the other necessities for daily life takes place according to time-honored techniques with tools and simple machines powered by humans or domesticated animals. But to an increasing extent the industrial system has invaded even such outposts through its incessant need for raw materials, labor, and, finally, markets for its products. As this process continues, it becomes more and more difficult to find societies which have not, in one way or another, been affected by it, and anthropologists must pay attention to the larger system if they expect to understand its subunits and the ways in which the latter maintain themselves or adapt to the changes going on all about them.

The mechanisms by which the rural citizens of the developing nations have become incorporated into the larger industrial system are many, but one which has been common in several parts of the world is that in which some individuals sell their labor on the open market at a site outside of their usual territory, which thus necessitates their absence from the domestic scene for some portion of their adult lives. Such activity — usually referred to as migratory wage labor — inevitably has an impact upon the native sociocultural system. At the very least, it brings cash and new ideas into the community. But it may have other repercussions that are more fundamental, although less obvious, depending upon the particular circumstances involved.

Some migrants, for example, may never return, electing to remain in the work site — often a city — permanently. This, then, becomes an integral part of the phenomenon of urbanization, about which we still know little in reference to the non-Western developing societies, but which has lately drawn the attention of many anthropologists and others. The emphasis in such studies is usually upon the urban scene itself — the adaptation of the migrant to "urbanism as a way of life," or the development of new types of urban social structures as part of the general transition to industrialization (Fried 1959; Hammel 1964; Lewis 1961; Mangin 1959).

The effects of such migration upon the home village have been either ignored or treated in the light of breakdown or disorganization of the original social structure — usually with presumed or real effects upon the mental health of the inhabit-

ants. It has also sometimes been assumed that rural-to-urban
migration simply drains off the surplus population from the
countryside, thus leaving the latter to its more or less pristine
folk existence. It is generally understood, of course, that there
will be an increased demand in the countryside for manufactured goods and an unquenchable thirst for the excitement of
urban living — which desires spur further outward migration,
especially of the younger people. In fact, the wonder might be
that such societies persist at all after migration once gets
started!

There is, however, much evidence that in many societies
temporary migration for the purpose of securing work has not
led to any significant permanent loss of population, and, as in
much of the Pacific, urbanization has not always been an early
concomitant of the spread of the industrial system. Furthermore, cash cropping, home industries, or the introduction of a
factory into a native village will also lead to modernization,
but probably along different routes than that resulting from
migration. And, finally, it seems that the nature of the migratory pattern itself varies with the opportunities for employment, the needs of the natives, and other factors, and that this
variability is of importance in assessing the effect of the migration upon the society.

The literature concerning the effect of industrialization
upon traditional societies reminds me of the descriptions of the
elephant by the proverbial six blind men — it all depends
upon where you focus your empirical research. Despite the
fact that there are many variables to be considered, it strikes
me that blindness (or shortsightedness) has prevented many
investigators from standing off at a distance great enough to
perceive the system as a whole, through both time and space.
When we do this, certain things become clearer, and we realize
that there are likely to be regular and repetitive processes involved in the adaptation of such societies to the modern world.
Furthermore, two apparently different situations may in fact
represent separate phases or aspects of the same process. Thus,

the study of urbanization is incomplete without recognition of the fact that this is merely one aspect of the process of migratory wage labor. Yet not all migrants become city dwellers, and many of them become so only after a lifetime of intermittent, temporary periods of work during which they remain closely tied to their villages.

There are, as I have suggested elsewhere (Gonzalez 1961), several patterns frequently lumped together under the general category "migratory wage labor," which might better be distinguished if we are interested in analyzing the effects of these patterns upon other social structures. However, it is probable that all of the types suggested might be shown to have adaptive effects under some circumstances. Although the specific structures involved will vary tremendously, I suggest that, from the point of view of the society furnishing migratory wage labor, all of the different patterns serve to accomplish the following:

1. *Articulation to the larger society.* These patterns provide a means for securing selected goods, services, and ideas from the modern world, while at the same time insulating the bulk of the population, as well as the social structure itself, from the shock of total immersion.

2. *Maintenance of optimum population size.* Migration drains off any excess population which may itself be a result of improved medical and agricultural technology introduced from the outside. This is the effect not only of permanent removal to the cities or elsewhere, but also of the temporary or seasonal types of labor which take only a portion of the total adult laboring force at any given time. The latter permit a larger number of persons to be supported within the context of the indigenous socioeconomic system. The determination of what size is "optimum" must be made in accordance with the particular conditions extant in each society and will depend, in part, upon the value judgments of the members of that society.

3. *Maintenance of traditional societies with low economic productivity.* Migratory wage labor may be a means of securing income to support the *status quo* of societies with faltering

indigenous economies. Because of increased population pressure, competition for land, destruction of natural resources, or other factors, a society may find itself on the brink of total disaster. In such cases, income from outside sources may serve to bolster the economy and the social system based upon it, which might otherwise be forced to adopt new productive techniques, acquire new lands, or make some other basic change in order to survive.

It should be pointed out that all three of these adaptive consequences of migration are probably only temporary; it appears that, eventually, migratory wage labor and the societies it manages to maintain for a time both disappear under the steam roller of industrialization. From this point of view, migratory wage labor might be considered as evidence of impending social disorganization for the home society. However, it is here suggested that these patterns may also be viewed as mechanisms for *maintaining* a traditional society with only slight modifications long after the initial impact of industrialization has hit the larger system of which that society is a part. In addition, migratory wage labor may also smooth the way toward eventual complete dependence upon the industrial system by stimulating the development of new social structures and value systems more compatible with that system. The problem of why some societies seem to have survived relatively unchanged for several generations *in spite of* continual contacts with the outside world through migratory wage labor is, then, no longer meaningful. Instead, we might consider the possibility that some societies have survived for generations within the general framework of advancing industrialization *because of* migratory wage labor, which serves to help the rural society adjust itself to changing conditions that might otherwise destroy it.

The following study sets forth the historical development of wage labor among the Black Carib and attempts to indicate some of its effects upon the social structure of the home villages — particularly in regard to the family and household. Although there have been extensive revisions and rearrangement of parts, plus an updating of the theoretical and cross-cultural discussions to include reference to recent pertinent publications, it should be stressed that the general point of view and the analysis and conclusions are basically the same as those in the original dissertation. In fact, the conclusions seem to have been further supported by later field work, both by me in the Carib area and by others elsewhere. Since this monograph was completed in 1958, many important works have appeared which discuss or contribute more data relevant to the issues dealt with here. I have attempted to include references to such materials at appropriate places in the text, and have made some changes in terminology in order to conform to usages which have now become general, or which I consider to be more adequate than those in the earlier manuscript. However, it has not seemed either necessary or appropriate to include extensive discussions relating my data to these newer studies. Although some of them have gone far beyond me in analyzing certain aspects of West Indian social structure, none of them appear to contradict any of my materials, and none of them have concentrated upon the role of migratory wage labor in historical perspective as a major factor in the development of what I have called consanguineal households.

The field research upon which the present study is based was done from July 1, 1956, to July 1, 1957, on the Caribbean coast of Central America. The center of operations was at Livingston, Guatemala, a town of about twenty-five hundred persons, of whom nearly eighteen hundred are of the ethnic group known as Black Carib to anthropologists, or as *Garifuna* to themselves. More commonly, one hears the term *Moreno* (Spanish — brunette, or "dark one"), by which the other residents of the area refer to the Black Caribs. Here I will, for brevity, use simply "Carib."

From October 10 to November 5, I toured the Carib villages of British Honduras, visiting as well a number of non-

Carib Negro villages in the same area for purposes of comparison. A week was spent in the capital city of Belize doing research in the archives and libraries and gathering data on the Creole culture of the country. This visit was followed by a return to one village later in November to witness an important Carib festival, known as "Settlement Day," which commemorates the supposed date of the first Carib migration to British Honduras from the Republic of Honduras.

In February, 1957, I went to the Republic of Honduras and visited several Carib towns and villages along the north coast of that country. After this tour, which lasted five weeks, I spent four days in the capital, Tegucigalpa, doing archival research.

The remainder of the time I was in Livingston, although I made frequent trips to the nearby port of Barrios, which provides employment and residence for many Caribs, permanent for some and temporary for the great majority. Many of the latter call Livingston their home. During these trips I interviewed numerous officials of the United Fruit Company, especially Sr. Don Eduardo Solares, Director of Labor Relations, and Ray Usher, a native of British Honduras. I also visited many of the homes of Caribs in Puerto Barrios, and observed and talked with men working on the docks.

Several different methods of obtaining data were used, depending upon the kind of information sought and the circumstances under which I was working. In Livingston, where I rented a small native house in a Carib compound, I lived in close association with one extended family. Gradually I increased my sphere of operations, making friends first within the neighborhood and among the kindred of the family with whom I lived. Later I extended my observations to include people who were from distant barrios and were unrelated to my hostess' kin. At various times and with various people I attended festivals; went to the fields to observe planting, cultivation, and harvest; attended meetings of women's clubs; went to funerals and wakes; attended the Catholic church and talked often with the priest; attended dances; visited schools; and talked with various municipal officials, such as the mayor, the port captain, and schoolteachers. In addition, I held many interviews with selected informants on various topics which do not lend themselves to participation techniques, such as witchcraft, history, sex life, translations of Carib songs and stories, and the like. One area in which my participation was limited because of my sex was that of fishing. Therefore, I only interviewed men on this subject and observed seine fishing and night crabbing from the shore. Nor was I able to attend meetings of the men's clubs, so information on these also depends entirely on interviews.

On my trip into British Honduras I stayed with a Creole family in Belize, and so was able to observe patterns of life in such a family at first hand; in other villages I stayed with Carib families. This gave me comparative material on family life to supplement and check my observations in Livingston, where I lived only with the family from which I rented my house. Although I stayed alone in a separate house, it was situated within a compound in such a way that I was able to observe the daily life of members of four other households.

A map and a census were made of the town of Livingston; the statistics presented herein are derived primarily from these sources or from municipal records from that town.

In British Honduras I visited the grapefruit cannery outside of Stann Creek and interviewed officials there regarding employment practices, number of Caribs employed, and wages paid. Such information was also obtained at a lumber camp that employed numerous Caribs. At that time these were virtually the *only* enterprises in that colony hiring large numbers of employees.

In Honduras, I talked with officials in each port town, including Cortes, Tela, and La Ceiba, as well as in La Lima, the headquarters of the Honduras division of the United Fruit Company. In all towns, including Livingston, I interviewed non-Caribs belonging to various ethnic groups — such as Ladinos, Creoles,[1] North Americans, and Europeans — to obtain information on their attitudes toward Caribs and also on their own patterns of culture. Two groups with whom I did not establish rapport were the East Indian group living in Livingston and the Guatemalan Indians of Kekchi speech, who did not live in that town but used it as a market center.

These details will permit the reader to evaluate more concretely the information obtained and the generalizations made. In the body of the text, unless stated otherwise, specific details given are from the town of Livingston. My tours through other areas provided some comparative material, but only on selected topics, for I never stayed long enough in any given town to be able to describe with certainty all the existing culture patterns. Nevertheless, my observations and questions, based on fresh experience in Livingston, enabled me to learn much in a short time at each locality I visited. Beyond this, the survey broadened my outlook in regard to Livingston itself.

I wish to acknowledge the assistance given me in the form of a grant by the Henry L. and Grace Doherty Foundation, which made this research possible. A supplementary grant for equipment to be used during the field work was made by the Department of Anthropology of the University of Michigan.

The United Fruit Company cooperated in facilitating contact with employees in all divisions visited and in some cases helped with transportation within Honduras and Guatemala and in housing at their various stations. I would especially like to thank Sr. Eduardo Solares, of Puerto Barrios, and his wife, Concha, who were a constant source of friendship, information, hospitality, and general assistance on my frequent visits to that town.

The hospitality and willingness to cooperate of my numer-

---

[1] I define the term "Creole" according to common usage in British Honduras as any person born in the colony of Negro or mixed Negro descent. Ladinos are here defined as persons of Latin American, non-Indian culture, who may or may not be Mestizos from the point of view of race. For the most complete discussion of this culture, see Adams 1956.

ous Carib hosts and hostesses in all the villages visited facilitated my work and will always be appreciated. Although I cannot mention each by name here, I wish to acknowledge my debt of gratitude to all who helped me.

I would also like to thank the following of my former professors and colleagues, all of whom read the manuscript in part or in whole and offered valuable comments and criticisms: Professors David F. Aberle, Richard K. Beardsley, Lloyd A. Fallers, Clifford Geertz, Ross N. Pearson, Marshall D. Sahlins, Richard F. Salisbury, David M. Schneider, William T. Stuart, and Leslie A. White. Dr. Elman R. Service provided much-needed moral and professional encouragement during the time I was in the field, and his constant criticism and advice were much appreciated. Dr. June Helm was of great assistance in the final revision, helping me to "modernize" the presentation without changing its essential point. Although I owe much to all of these, none should be held responsible for the opinions and interpretations offered in the text.

Finally, grateful acknowledgment is made to Audrey Cawley Mills and Anne Chapman Baudez, both of whom gave generously of their time and talents in preparing the manuscript.

~~~~~~~~~~~~

CONTENTS

~~~~~~~~~~~~

ILLUSTRATIONS

BLACK CARIB HOUSEHOLD STRUCTURE

A Study of Migration and Modernization

One

≈≈≈≈≈≈≈≈≈≈≈≈≈≈≈≈≈≈≈≈≈≈≈≈≈≈≈≈≈≈≈

STATEMENT OF PROBLEM
AND HYPOTHESES

≈≈≈≈≈≈≈≈≈≈≈≈≈≈≈≈≈≈≈≈≈≈≈≈≈≈≈≈≈≈≈

T HE central concern of this study is the description and
analysis of the type of household organization that char-
acterizes Black Carib culture. The particular forms involved
merit close study because they appear to exist in various societies around the world. In some cases, their coexistence as a
type has not been recognized by persons examining the culture; in other cases, researchers have recognized and studied
the type, each worker attempting to define it and account for
its existence.

I am here using the word "type" in a technical sense much
as it has been used by some archaeologists in referring to culture types (see Willey and Phillips 1958:12–16). That is, a
type is a distinctive association or clustering of certain social
or cultural forms. Ethnographically, a type is identifiable in
particular time and space, as when I .speak of Black Carib
household organization in 1956. Theoretically, however, a

type may be said to recur whenever and wherever the necessary preconditions are present.

The type to be discussed here, as exemplified in Black Carib society, consists of a series of household forms, each of which is identified by the composition of the domestic group, and especially by the nature of the kinship bonds linking adult men and women in such groups. For example, if the members of the household are related through a series of consanguineal ties, and no two members are bound together in an affinal relationship, we have what is here termed a "consanguineal household." The existence of an affinal tie between any two members places the household in the class here termed "affinal." Within each of these primary classes there may be great variety in household composition, as will be illustrated later in more detail.

At this point it should be emphasized that although we are primarily concerned with consanguineal households — what they are, how they come into being, and how they function — none of the societies dealt with here have it as their *only* form. Affinal households of various kinds are always found as alternate structures. Indeed, an important characteristic of the type is the fact that households change from one form to another under different kinds of stimuli. Thus, we are not justified in taking merely the most frequent form as typical of the society as a whole. Rather, our type consists of a series of household forms, ranging from the small conjugal family household to that in which members are bound by consanguineal ties alone. The various forms are unstable and sensitive to certain pressures under which they may readily change into a different form.

The only household form in the series which may be somewhat unusual is the consanguineal household. In the chapters which follow I shall attempt to deal thoroughly with this form in an effort to contribute toward the understanding of its nature. In addition, I shall endeavor to show under what circumstances one form within the type may change to another, and, more broadly, what characteristics of the society as a whole operate to maintain the stability of the type through time.

In previous studies, all dealing with Afro-American societies, at least three different prime explanatory factors have been suggested: (1) local economic position of males, (2) survival of conditions imposed by slavery, and (3) African heritage. To clarify the problem, I will outline the viewpoint behind each of these three modes of explanation.

R. T. Smith, in dealing with the Negroes of British Guiana, whose social organization apparently includes this type of household organization, has used the term "matrifocal" to identify the type, thereby emphasizing the role played by the female. He says that this "matrifocal system of domestic relations and household grouping . . . can be regarded as the obverse of the marginal nature of the husband-father role." And, further, "there is a correlation between the nature of the husband-father role and the role of men in the economic system" (R. T. Smith 1956:221). He goes on to suggest that the low position of the Negro man in the class-color hierarchy in British Guiana limits him to jobs that offer low remuneration and that require him to be absent from his home village much of the time. This situation is also typical of the other societies noted that exhibit the matrifocal system, so that Smith's explanation has a great deal to recommend it. However, it seems to have certain deficiencies as a total answer, since it does not explain why matrifocality is not found in all societies where there is migrant wage labor with low remuneration and low social status of males, most notably, many societies in Africa and Melanesia.

Another theory that has many adherents takes particular note of the fact that this type of household organization is found almost universally among the New World Negro. E. F. Frazier (1942, 1948) held to the view that this system became prominent during the period of slavery. As slaves, men and women were usually discouraged from forming permanent conjugal alliances; if they did, they were likely to be torn away from each other at any time and sold separately. Children, on the other hand, especially when very young, were sold with their mothers. This association tended to increase the intensity of the bond between mother and child. The slaveholders usually looked to the woman as the head of the house, allotting the weekly or yearly rations to her to distribute as she saw fit. Children were given the name of their mother, not their father, and the mother alone (or another woman acting as mother) was held responsible for their upbringing and discipline.

This viewpoint holds that one of the consequences of the system was the emergence of a double standard in which legal, monogamous marriage was regarded as the correct pattern of behavior for the white man, but not necessarily for the black. In fact, slaves were sometimes encouraged to change sex partners frequently, in the belief that this would increase their fecundity. The present family form of Negroes in the New World, usually characterized in some degree by unstable marriage and a strong mother-child bond, is considered by adherents to this view to be a direct result of the period of slavery. Others besides Frazier who support this view include Campbell (1943), Henriques (1953), King (1945), Myrdal (1944), Powdermaker (1939), and Woofter (1930).

M. J. Herskovits and some of his students, on the other hand, relate the whole system to historical antecedents in Africa. Herskovits pointed out that in West Africa, the area of origin of most New World Negroes, the family pattern, though usually connected with patrilineal or double descent, most often involved polygyny, with separate households for each wife and her children. Men divided their time among their several wives, and as a result each woman was ultimately in charge of her particular household. The children of each woman developed extremely strong ties to each other and to her but not to their half-siblings with different mothers. The economic system in which the women marketed their garden produce and had the right to spend the profits as they saw fit is also seen by Herskovits as providing an antecedent pattern for the New World to follow. These previous circumstances, combined with the situation of slavery in the New World, produced a new pattern, which according to Herskovits, was a reinterpretation of African customs to fit a new social environment. (See Herskovits 1937, 1941, 1943, 1946; Bascom 1941.)

A few other minor theories have been presented, though they have received comparatively little notice. Among these, the most interesting and possibly the most fruitful is that which relates the solidarity of the consanguineal group to a general situation of land shortage (Clarke 1953, 1957; Cohen 1954; Cumper 1954). Briefly, it is suggested that where land shortage becomes acute in an agricultural society, and where few economic alternatives are provided, the sibling group which inherits the land in common (typical throughout the West Indies) will remain together at the expense of any affinal ties they might have contracted. The binding force is the fear of losing one's rights to share in the family land. This theory will be discussed at greater length below.

Each of these theories is interesting, but none explains all the facts at hand. Another limitation is that each one treats the New World Negro pattern as though it were unique. Hence none provides illumination for other societies exhibiting this type of system. R. T. Smith (1956), who does use comparative material from non-Negro societies, has cases which do not seem to be truly comparable, for reasons which will be dealt with in a later chapter.

Since this monograph was originally written, several persons have written articles expanding and reinterpreting some of the ideas in it. In another publication (Gonzalez 1965) I have dealt with Peter Kunstadter's paper (1963) in which he wrongly assumed that I was dealing with the matrifocal family rather than with the consanguineal household. He cites the Nayar of the Malabar Coast as occupying an extreme position on a hypothetical continuum of matrifocality. As I will elaborate further below, there seem to me to be important differences between the Nayar case and that of the Black Carib which make them not truly comparable (see below, page 14). However, Kunstadter agreed that an imbalance in the sex ratio and the existence of a money economy were important factors in accounting for female-headed households.

Keith F. Otterbein also assumed that I was dealing with matrifocal, or female-headed, households rather than with consanguineal households, and proceeded to elaborate upon what he calls my "male absenteeism hypothesis" (1965:68). He correctly points out that the mating system is an important variable, and also suggests that "economic and demographic factors — in particular, opportunities to earn and save money and the sex ratio — are the major determinants of Caribbean family systems."

Perhaps the most important recent work on Caribbean family systems is that of M. G. Smith. He too emphasizes that the mating system must be considered in order to achieve an understanding of the patterns of household and family composition, and also presents considerable evidence to show that collateral relatives — most especially those on the mother's side — are at least as important as the mother's mother or grandmother in the web of cooperative relationships on the domestic scene. However, his "explanation" of the family system is essentially tautological, in that he repeatedly refers it back to the mating system, which itself is not explained, except in historical terms. He explicitly rejects the possibility that demographic, ecological, or economic factors operate as determining factors (1962b:203–9).

In all instances in which we find the system under discussion, the society is living, as it were, on the fringes of Western civilization. It is locally distinguished from the larger society of which it forms a part, existing as a small in-group with some distinctive traditions and customs, though economically dependent upon the larger society. The culturally patterned social relationships are of two kinds: those which take their sanctions from the smaller society alone, and those which derive from the larger Western background. Adherence to the latter generally yields higher prestige, but since the total economic and social configuration often makes it impossible for all members of the society to maintain behavior of this sort. there also exists another distinct pattern, which is socially approved only by the members of the in-group itself. The consanguineal household, with all the social relationships that the term implies, is here held to be such a complex, which arises in certain systems as a functional result of the group's attempt to adapt to a modern economy in which production is primarily for gain rather than for use.

Moreover, the material available on tribes in East, Central, and South Africa, as well as in certain parts of Melanesia, and on American Indian groups, which are today in the process of adapting to Western culture through the mechanism of wage labor, is most significant for our problem because these groups do *not* seem to form consanguineal household organizations. Certain features of their changed kinship systems and other aspects of their altered social organization are in some respects parallel to those found among the Black Carib. Common characteristics are a high rate of divorce, less respect shown toward things old and traditional, increase in premarital and extramarital sexual alliances, increase in number of "illegitimate" children, and increased relative importance of women in the domestic economic system. Nevertheless, these conditions are not sufficient to group such systems with the consanguineal systems here being analyzed. As we shall see, a distinctive series of household forms with definite characteristics constitutes the type, a type which has the advantage of alleviating or compensating for the disruptive effects of ongoing changes in the economic system.

Consanguineal systems are limited in their distribution in the world to societies whose traditional culture has been forcibly changed or dissolved through the intervention of forces from the Western world, or to societies of mixed-bloods who have found themselves occupying a position between the two cultures from which they derived. Such groups have characteristics different from those of the larger society within which they are living, yet they cannot be termed primitive, peasant, folk, or any other such designation which implies a traditional basis for the society. The mere fact of miscegenation does not bring this about, of course. Rather, such a society must also be placed in the position of having to adapt to an economy dependent upon industrialization through the mechanism of migrant wage labor, while being denied full admission to the industrial society as a whole, both as a class and as individuals. From the point of view of the urban or more modern segments of nations where these societies exist today, the latter may seem to be "traditional" in that they are not *fully* adapted to or incorporated into the industrial system. I have used the term "traditional" in this sense in the preface, but I feel it is important to make some distinction here between those sociocultural systems which still retain a certain degree of *structural* self-sufficiency, usually supported by strong ideological sanctions, and those whose more shallow cultural roots do not provide them with such traditional integration mechanisms. In a sense, a capacity for change is built into these systems, which must continually adapt themselves or be annihilated. I have chosen to call these societies "neoteric" [1] in this study in order to distinguish them from all types of traditional societies.

The process of industrialization has created many such societies throughout the world. These groups have often been referred to as "disorganized," "broken," or "disrupted." Such terms, regardless of what is actually meant by them, imply a value judgment which has no place in an objective appraisal of social organization. In addition, they tend to obscure the fact that these societies are functioning, thriving units, the study of which may bring forth many new social facts and theories to contribute to our understanding of the nature of society. It is

[1] "Recent in origin; modern; new," according to *Webster's New International Dictionary*.

true that such societies may be disorganized from the point of view of the sociocultural system from which the members or their ancestors derived, but in terms of the present time these groups have achieved a new equilibrium. They were created by the very conditions to which they are adapted, so we must study these conditions as well as the societies themselves to understand the new organizations. It is not necessary that a society lose its traditional character immediately upon entrance into the orbit of industrial economy. The process may be slow and gradual, in which case the final result will probably be much different than in the neoteric societies here being discussed.

Examination of economic systems in which the primary source of cash is migratory wage labor, rather than either stationary wage labor or production for sale (whether of crops or handicrafts), reveals some important points which have bearing on the present problem.

Elsewhere I have reviewed the literature on the subject of migratory wage labor. I have attempted to show that this term includes several essentially different patterns of behavior which are not strictly comparable in terms of their effects on the social organization of the home village (Gonzalez 1961).

I have isolated the type which I call "recurrent migration" as the only one which appears to coexist with the consanguineal household. Other types include (1) seasonal migration, (2) temporary, nonseasonal migration (illustrated by the Melanesian pattern described in Chapter VI), (3) continuous migration (for example, United States fruit pickers), and (4) permanent removal (such as is now occurring in parts of Africa where migrants break all ties with the home village and become stabilized in town). All of these types will be further discussed and illustrated in Chapter VI.

There are, however, several characteristics of recurrent migration which have bearing on the initial statement of the problem. First, the work is often at some distance from the man's home, requiring him to be absent from the household for more than just a part of every day. In some cases he may return fairly frequently, that is, once a week, but in others he may be away for years. Often the employment is only intermittently available and calls for unskilled labor, so that no job security is possible. The laborer may find himself forced to move great distances from one labor center to another as the demand shifts.

The second characteristic is the remuneration received for this type of work. With the advent of labor unions, rising nationalism in some countries, and the increase in industrialization seen everywhere, real wages for unskilled and semi-skilled labor are slowly rising. Big business, however, still often considers that the native does not need the same wage paid to Westerners for the same work. For most of the societies with which we are here concerned, the only wage-labor jobs open have been in so-called "exploitative" industries. Some of these have been in colonial outposts of large empires, while others have been in independent republics that have been forced through economic need to permit large foreign corporations to come in and develop an industry. In either case, a cheap labor supply has been one of the factors consistently appealing to employers, who have fostered mechanisms for perpetuating these conditions. As the standards of living in these societies changed and as the native became more and more dependent upon wage labor as a source of livelihood, his needs for cash increased but his wages did not. These factors too have contributed to the maintenance of the type of household system here described.

In recurrent migration men make irregular journeys of varying durations to obtain wage labor throughout their productive years. In most cases their wives and families are left behind in the native villages. The man in his husband-father role is thus absent a good deal of the time, and the woman cannot depend upon him for anything but sporadic assistance in domestic affairs. A woman may have several consanguineally related males (especially brothers, mother's brothers, and sons)

to whom she may turn for help in child rearing, housebuilding, and clearing of fields. Although at any given time some of these men will be absent, usually there will be at least one upon whom she may call.

This economic situation does not permit the smaller society to maintain permanent nuclear families headed by a male, for in most cases he must be absent a good deal of the time; he probably does not earn enough cash to furnish the entire support of his family, and he leaves the household shorthanded during his absence. Neither does this situation permit families to maintain themselves when only one adult female is present, for if the population is to survive at all, the women must generally supplement the cash income of the males. Very often they do this by growing garden produce — for home consumption or sale, or both. Occasionally, too, the women may find opportunities to earn cash through other means, but it should be noted that in most cases the locations of the men's and the women's work are separate. This necessitates household groups of a size and composition sufficient to carry out the domestic functions when both the adult male and the adult female are absent. A nucleus bound together by consanguineal ties of one sort or another seems to be more effective and more stable under these conditions than those consisting of adults bound by affinity. This statement has an empirical basis, but why this situation should exist under the conditions specified will become apparent in later chapters where neoteric systems are described and analyzed.

As will be seen when we review the social relations among members of consanguineal households, many features parallel those of social systems based on matrilineality. The close comparison of traits of the consanguineal household with those of matrilineal systems falls outside the scope of the present work. However, on the basis of preliminary comparison, the details of which need not be presented here, it seems most likely that the similarities are only superficial.

The classic case of the Nayar should be mentioned at this

point, for not only was this group characterized by matrilineal descent, but their households were organized strictly along consanguineal lines. In a sense, it might not be inappropriate to state that the Nayar carried matrilineality and the consanguineal household to an extreme unknown elsewhere, as Kunstadter has suggested (1963).

However, it should be emphasized that virtually *all* households among the Nayar were consanguineal, being composed of a group of women related through the maternal line, their children, and the brothers of the women, the latter being present only part of the time (Gough 1952:85; Mencher 1962). Furthermore, this household type was the *ideal*, as well as the most frequently found unit. In this regard the Nayar form a special case, essentially different from the Black Carib, for example, among whom the consanguineal household exists as an acceptable, but less prestigious, alternative to the ideal nuclear family household.

It is true that in both societies males were absent from the home villages intermittently — for purposes of warfare in the case of the Nayar, and for wage labor among the Carib. If we consider only this factor, we might posit a relationship between absence of males and the presence of the consanguineal household. However, when we consider the nondomestic elements of each sociocultural system, important differences appear which suggest that we are not dealing with comparable units. The Nayar male gained status in the society at large through his participation in ritual, jural, and economic activities, all of which were intimately connected with the matrilineage. Conversely, the matrilineage, or segment of a lineage, could not afford to lose males, who performed many functions necessary to the maintenance of the group as a whole. The consanguineal household among the Nayar can only be understood in relation to the matrilineal organization of the entire society, in which this particular type of dwelling unit was highly valued. Furthermore, Nayar society operated in such a way that the ideal type of household unit was in fact achieved consistently.

In Black Carib society, on the other hand, several different household forms exist, each of which appears to be functional under different circumstances. The consanguineal form seems to be relatively recent, and cannot be considered as the ideal form, even though at the time of the present study 40 per cent of all households conformed to this type (see Table 3, p. 68). In spite of the fact that the nuclear family household is the ideal, it appears that the economic foundations of Carib society are such that the majority of the members of the society find this ideal difficult to achieve and *maintain*. The consanguineal household seems to be formed by default rather than as a positive mechanism oriented toward reinforcing solidarity among members of a matrilineage in which the loss of males would be fatal to the system. Males are, of course, important in many ways to a Black Carib household, but it matters little to the unit as a whole whether its male members occupy the role of brother-uncle or husband-father.

It is necessary to ask whether a matrilineal system might not eventually emerge from a consanguineal system, for the latter is usually (if not always) bilateral with a strong matrilateral bias. One of the most important functions of descent groups in general is that they may act as corporate groups. Thus, such a group can own or manage property, including land, water resources, grazing rights, and the like. It can and does have functions in the legal and political spheres, allocating rights, controlling behavior through threat of loss of these rights, regulating marriage and inheritance of property in such a way that property remains within the circle of a limited number of people without being diffused so widely that it becomes either less productive or too small an asset to be of value to any given individual. The descent group, then, has many more functions than merely providing an individual with a way to keep track of his relatives.

If I am correct in stating that consanguineal households as

an alternate type are found only in those societies which are already incorporated into a larger society with state organization, and, furthermore, if these societies have at the time of their entrance into those wider systems been so uprooted that former traditions have been discarded, then descent groups would never come into being simply because there would be no function for them to fulfill. In addition, such societies are constantly confronted by the value system of the Western world, and the ideals learned from it also channel these societies away from matriliny, a system quite foreign to the modern Western way of thinking and behaving.

In summary, the major hypothesis of this study is that the consanguineal household is an alternate type of domestic group that develops during the process of acculturation of neoteric societies in which the primary mechanism of Westernization is recurrent migratory wage labor with low remuneration.

Two

~~~~~~

HISTORICAL BACKGROUND
OF BLACK CARIB SOCIETY

~~~~~~

THE Black Carib are a hybrid population with a hybrid culture stemming from the escaped Negroes and the Red, or
Island, Caribs who inhabited St. Vincent's Island in the Lesser
Antilles during the seventeenth and eighteenth centuries. D. M.
Taylor (1951), who has provided us with the only published
monographic treatment of this group in recent years, includes
a brief historical résumé up to the end of the eighteenth century.
I will draw from his account for this early period and supplement
it with data from my own research for the nineteenth and twentieth centuries.

Taylor's account of the gradual infiltration of Negroes into
St. Vincent's Island states that Negroes were living there soon
after the French and English moved into the area (1625). A
document dated 1667 mentions that the island contained Indians and some Negroes from the loss of two Spanish ships in
1635. Shortly after the first Negroes arrived, others — mostly

runaway slaves from nearby islands, especially from Barba-
does — began arriving. It appears that St. Vincent was becoming known as a harbor for fugitive slaves.⌐

⌐After continual warfare over the ownership of the islands in
the area, a treaty was signed in 1660 by which the French and
English guaranteed to the Caribs perpetual possession of Dominica and St. Vincent, the two islands still remaining to them
at that time. By this date there must have been many Negroes
living on each island, for from 1676 we have a document stating that St. Vincent then contained three thousand Negroes.
Still, it is not clear, at least from Taylor's account, whether
this treaty pertained to the Red Carib Indians alone, or
whether the Blacks and Reds were considered to be just one
group. Later evidence makes the second view less probable.

In 1683 the English attacked both Dominica and St. Vincent,
massacring many people and destroying houses and canoes.
Taylor, quoting Sieur de La Borde, tells us that at this time the
Negroes were as powerful as the Indians; such a statement indicates that as yet they were two separate groups. He says,
"Some [Negroes] are maroons or taken in war, and these are the
slaves of the Caribs, whom they call *tamu*, 'captive'; but most
come from some Flemish or Spanish ship which was wrecked
nearby their island" (1951:21). This statement suggests that
there were at this time two ethnic groups, the Caribs and the
Blacks, who probably carried on intermittent warfare which involved the capture of slaves. This description indicates that the
Caribs, at any rate, had Negro slaves, and from what we know
of slavery among these people, the captives probably lived
among them as Indians and even intermarried with them.

In 1700 we have evidence recorded by Jean-Baptiste Labat,
who visited the islands in that year. He tells us that the Negroes
had become quite powerful on St. Vincent, and that the Caribs
feared and resented them. The Negroes had forced the Caribs to
relinquish some lands to them, and made a practice of kidnaping
their women. On the other hand, this same author describes his
arrival in St. Vincent by saying that their ship was met by Caribs

and Negroes, all of whom were attired in similar dress and paint. He notes, however, that in spite of their attire, it was not difficult to distinguish the Caribs from the Negroes because of the hair form; and in addition they were differentiated by "the look of their heads, by their eyes, their mouths, and their corpulence, in all of which respects the ones differ greatly from the other" (Taylor 1951:23).

This seemingly contradictory evidence need not present such a mystery. We already know that the Caribs held many Negroes captive among them, and very likely the process of intermixture had been going on for at least two generations (about seventy-five years had passed since the arrival of the first Negroes on the island). Therefore, the group which met the boat may well have been composed of only one of the political units then on the island — most likely the group usually then called "Caribs," the term "Negro," or "Blacks," being used to designate the other. But it is reasonable to assume that in spite of their political and possible ethnic differences, these groups quite probably had interbred to a considerable extent.

In 1719 the French attempted to recapture the Negroes on the island of St. Vincent with the help of the latters' enemies, the Caribs. However, the Negroes, estimated to number four thousand, successfully avoided capture by retiring to the mountains and conducting guerrilla warfare from there. The Carib auxiliaries did not show up. Perhaps by this time there were too few of them, or they may have feared reprisals by the Negroes, who obviously were very powerful. Also, of course, there is the possibility that the Caribs by now had allied themselves with their former enemies and actually helped them against the French.

In 1773 the St. Vincent Caribs — who by now were mostly Negroes, and who, apparently for the first time, were referred to as the "Black Charaibes" — were driven into a reservation on the northern half of the island. However, during the period from 1779 to 1783, the Caribs, with the help of the French, regained control of the island. When the English returned again in 1783, they again restricted the Caribs to the reservation, an area which apparently was neither large enough nor sufficiently fertile to support the by now fairly sizable population. B. Edwards describes the Caribs at this time and says, "these were the black Charaibes, once the sole possessors of Saint Vincent, *by right of conquest from the original Charaibes*" [emphasis supplied] (Edwards 1818–19:4). Apparently, then, by 1783 the original Red Caribs had been killed off, had retired to Dominica, or had been assimilated, probably as individuals, into the groups once known as "Blacks," and now called "Black Carib." [1]

In 1795 the Black Caribs, at the instigation of the French, attempted once again to regain control of the island. But by 1796 they were completely defeated by the English and forced to surrender unconditionally. The Caribs were then estimated to number 5,000. The English, fearful of their demonstrated power, determined to remove them from the island of St. Vincent. Therefore, in 1797 they were landed on the island of Roatan off the coast of Trujillo, Honduras. It is difficult to understand the British reasoning which led to this move, especially in light of events which followed soon after. At that time the British were struggling to maintain every foothold possible on the Spanish Main. The Bay Islands, of which Roatan is the largest, comprised a strategic group which was to change hands many times between the British and Spanish. Perhaps it was thought that the belligerent Caribs would prevent outsiders from landing on this island, as they had attempted to do in St. Vincent. At any rate, two months after their arrival on Roatan, the Caribs peacefully turned over the island to the Spanish and set forth for the mainland, where they settled near Trujillo, Honduras.

The north or Caribbean coast of Honduras at that time was undeveloped commercially. There were no large plantations, and the population was sparse, consisting of small groups of

[1] Small enclaves of so-called "Red Caribs" have continued to exist as cultural entities down to the present time. These have been studied by D. M. Taylor (1938) and Banks (1956) on Dominica. Even these groups show a great amount of Negro admixture, though not nearly so much as the present-day Black Caribs.

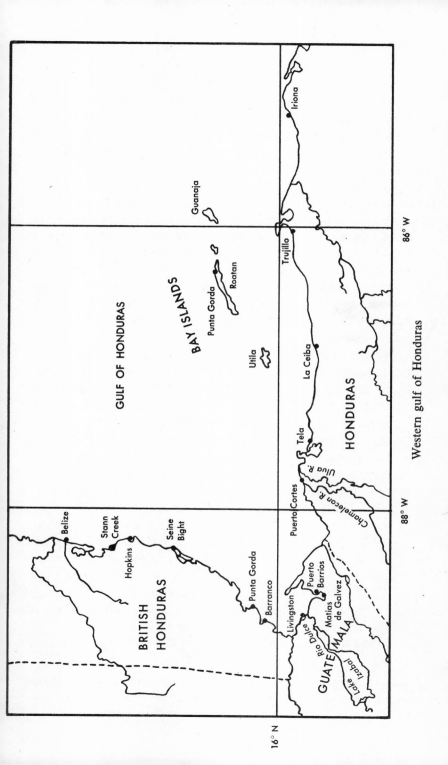

Western gulf of Honduras

Moskito Indians and refugee Negroes from Hispañola, both of which groups were engaged in fishing and subsistence horticulture. In addition there were Spaniards and Mestizos occupying the port towns of Trujillo, Cortes (formerly Puerto Caballo), and Omoa.

⌈We know that approximately four thousand Caribs were deported to Roatan.⌉Of these, the greater number went to the mainland, but a small settlement remains today at Punta Gorda on the island of Roatan. In Trujillo, Honduras, there is a fairly large settlement of Caribs, and three small villages lie just west of that town. From the very beginning the Caribs had to disperse into smaller units in order to carry on their horticulture, since their technology was not sufficiently advanced to maintain four thousand people in one settlement in that tropical environment.

⌈We are unable to reconstruct the exact time when each present-day village was founded, but we know that the Caribs began moving up the coast as far as the colony of Belize by 1802.⌉During that year several entries in the records of the Magistrate's Meetings of the British colony referred to the Caribs. One, dated December 17, 1802, records the sentiments of A. Cunningham Esq., who recommended expulsion of all Caribs from the colony on the basis that, "as everyone knew," it was the Caribs who committed atrocities in Grenada and St. Vincent. Furthermore, "[we see] great danger in the presence in this Settlement, so far from assistance, of numerous Charibs, believed to the number of one hundred and fifty" (Burdon 1931:60). In 1807 the Superintendent to the Magistrates expressed his surprise "to find that, in spite of his warning that all Caribs must be viewed with suspicion, Caribs have been sent to man the lookout post on Cay Corker, which is one of the highest importance" (Burdon 1934:102).

At the Magistrates Meeting on July 11, 1811, the High Constable

directed to warn all Charibs [*sic*] who could not produce a Permit or Ticket from the Superintend [*sic*], to quit the settlement in 48 hours. Notice to be given to all Charibs arriving, through the Non Commissioned Officer to whom they report at the Fort upon arrival, that they would subject themselves to imprisonment by remaining in the Settlement more than Forty Eight Hours, without leave in writing from the Superintendent, as the Magistrates considered them a most Dangerous People" [*ibid.*: 146].

⌈Again, on July 16, 1811, at the Magistrate's Meeting it was "Ordered that the Charibs now in Gaol, or that might be taken up agreeable to the orders in the 11th instant, be sent away in any of their Country crafts as early as possible by the High Constable" (*ibid.*).⌉

If we now look at evidence from the Honduras archives, we find a note dated 1804 which points out that the government was aware of the fact that the Black Caribs had journeyed to Belize. Thus, "this government knows that the Black Caribs travel to Belize without being seen due to the fact that they are camped quite a distance from the port [Trujillo] on the point of Quemara . . . and after eight to fifteen days of absence they are seen again in their huts" (Vallejo 1893:123).[2] This note referred to the practice of carrying contraband, a business which goes on to this day.

In addition to smuggling, many Caribs went to the colony to work in the mahogany cuttings. A note from British Honduras dated 1830 mentions numerous Caribs — not British subjects — who were hired by the cutters to labor in their works. Thomas Young, traveling in 1839, repeatedly mentions the Carib mahogany workers who hired themselves out for five to six months or sometimes longer. "On expiration of their engagement, they return to their homes laden with useful articles, and invariably well dressed" (1847:124). He describes this dress and points out that it appears to be an attempt to

[2] ". . . sabe este Gobierno que los Negros Caribes pasan a dicho Walis [Belize] sin ser vistos por estar acampados algunos a largas distancias del puerto en punta de Quemara . . . y despues de ocho a quince dias de ausencia vuelven a parecer en sus chozas . . ." (my translation).

emulate the appearance of the Buckra (English) officers at
Belize (*ibid.*:122).

The records indicate that for several years the British attempted to expel these Caribs from the colony, believing them
to be an extremely dangerous and undesirable element.
Whether or not they ever succeeded in expelling them for a
time, the Caribs kept returning, and finally in 1857 lands at
Stann Creek were officially leased to the Caribs who had been
settled there from about 1820. It is probable that the towns of
Livingston (Guatemala), and Punta Gorda (British Honduras) were settled at about the same date.

At the present time the Black Caribs live in a series of
towns and villages along the Caribbean coast of Central
America from Stann Creek, British Honduras, in the north,
to Iriona, Honduras, in the south. A few Carib individuals,
some with their families, have moved to other regions, but the
area delineated above remains, both in their thoughts and in
actual fact, the effective extent of their settlement. All of these
villages are on the coast, most settlements being built about a
hundred yards back from the beach itself.

—There are two main types of settlement pattern. One consists
of a row of houses, each separated by a hundred feet or so, extending along the beach for as far as two miles. The other
type, more characteristic of the larger towns, consists of houses
laid out in a series of rows. Streets or wide paths running parallel to the beach separate the rows. Small gardens adjoin
many of the houses, but the main fields of each village lie inland from the town anywhere from fifteen minutes' to several
hours' distance on foot. In either type of settlement the beach
is usually lined with dugout canoes and large seines hung out
on poles to dry. Thus, the Carib village is situated between the
two sources upon which it has traditionally depended for a living. In front is the sea and its fish; to the rear is the lowland
tropical forest in which bitter manioc is cultivated by the
slash-and-burn method.

The smaller villages contain few, if any, non-Carib inhabitants, although occasionally one may find civil servants, such as school teachers or policemen, or perhaps a Catholic priest. Larger towns, once entirely Carib, have gradually been infiltrated by other ethnic groups, usually because of the town's strategic position for the development of business and industry along this coast. Thus, the towns of Stann Creek and Punta Gorda in British Honduras, and Livingston in Guatemala, now include barrios of Ladinos. The first two towns, in common with all the port towns of Honduras, also contain a considerable population of Negroes, while Livingston harbors a small group of East Indians, commonly known as "Coolies." In all of the port towns reside some North Americans and Europeans, as well as numerous middle-class Latin Americans. Most Caribs, at some point in their lives, come into contact with members of all of these groups, and each has influenced Carib culture in some degree.

In physical appearance the Carib differs little, if any, from other Negroid peoples in the area. Most non-Caribs who have lived in the area for any length of time insist that they can distinguish Caribs merely by looking at them. Some claim that the Carib is slightly lighter in color, that he has higher cheekbones, that he is somewhat shorter and stockier than the Negro.

In D. M. Taylor's opinion, "the physical appearance of the present Black Carib population of Central America, and its apparent homogeneity, warrant the assumption that the proportion of Indian to Negro blood in the original five thousand deportees was relatively slight" (1951:27). There is a certain amount of evidence from sources after 1800, however, that the Caribs were not physically as homogeneous as Taylor assumes.

Although it is true that, upon casual observation, the Caribs appear to be a relatively homogeneous population at the present time, we have the words of Thomas Young concerning them in 1842 —"Some being coal black, others again nearly as yellow as saffron" (1847:123) — and this could be said a whole generation after their arrival on the Honduran coast.

The Caribs themselves have traditions stating that when they arrived in Central America they were not nearly as Negroid as at present. Informants from British Honduras to Trujillo have told me that in former times they intermarried with Negroes. We know from Honduran documents that there were present in the Trujillo area so-called French Negroes from Santo Domingo, as well as a settlement of "English Negroes" but one league away from the town.[3] In 1804 the Spanish government expressed fear that the great number of Negroes in Trujillo would soon flood the entire coast (Vallejo 1893:123). Bard (1855:339) reports that Negroes had been present on the Moskito shore since 1704 at least, and that many of them had intermarried with the Indians and other natives living there.[4]

In my own records of genealogies I find numerous people among the Caribs who count a "pure Negro" in their recent ancestry. In fact, the partially historical, partially mythical account of the settling of Livingston, which informants place at about 1806, is said to have been led by a "Haitian" (Dominican?) Negro named Marco Sánchez Díaz. Descendants of this man, who has become somewhat of a culture hero, still live in Livingston today. Whether or not he was a Haitian, the story is important because it shows that the Caribs have had some history of cooperating with those "French Negroes" who we know were in Trujillo at the time of the Carib immigration.

In actuality, the differences seem to be primarily cultural. That is, the Carib speaks a different language, and because this tongue is learned first, he usually has an accent when speaking either Spanish or English. It is claimed that the Carib

[3] See Houdaille (1954) for a good description of these French Negroes in Central America.

[4] I quote Bard (pseudonym for E. G. Squier) here and elsewhere in this book. However, it should be noted that in several incidents recorded in his 1855 work, the events and words used to describe them bear remarkable resemblance to the narrative of Thomas Young, published in 1847. There is little doubt that Bard (Squier) actually visited the area in question; however, I have tried not to quote him in those incidents which might be questioned.

has a distinctive odor, something which my observations could never detect, but which, if true, also probably has a cultural basis. The Carib woman dresses in a different way from her Negro neighbors, and one who knows both groups well may detect a few different motor habits such as walking gait and stance. All of these, however, are purely subjective evaluations, and there exist no anthropometric data to substantiate or refute the claim that physical differences exist. The actual cultural differences bear little relationship to those which most of the non-Carib residents of the area believe exist. In fact, in many ways the Carib culture shares more with West Indian Negro cultures than it does with the Indians from whom they obtained their name and language (Solien 1959c). One reason that this fact is not always recognized by the casual observer, or even the professional, is that Caribs have preserved many West Indian culture traits which have long since disappeared among the Jamaicans and other West Indians who also inhabit this coast.

If the Black Carib, already a distinct group on arrival, were in British Honduras from 1800 on, as we have concluded, their culture must have been much influenced by contact with the Creole culture there. No thorough studies of this culture exist, unfortunately. However, intermarriage with Creoles and other Negro people along this coast, before the Carib were set apart in outcast status, may have intensified the Negroid physical features of the Black Carib. Although it has been thought that the Caribs were an entirely endogamous group since their arrival in Central America, I believe that this endogamy lies more in the realm of "ideal culture" than actual culture. Their present status as an outcast group, especially in the colony, and the fact that they tend to live in isolated communities stretched along the coast would seem to support the ideal of endogamy. I believe that the evidence indicates that they were not outcasts when they first arrived on this coast, at least not so far as other Negroid peoples were concerned. Rather, it appears that their status as such crystallized through the long process in

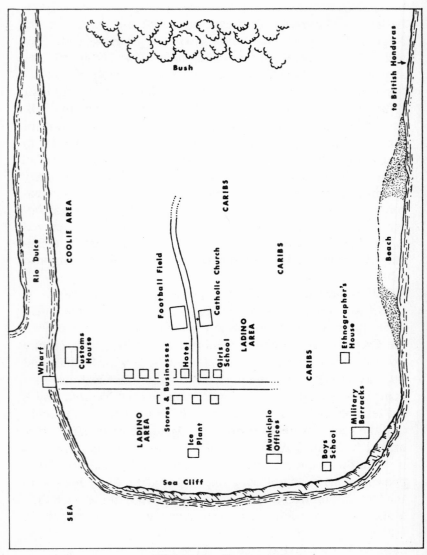

Livingston, Guatemala

which Caribs gradually came to be the preferred workers along this coast. Being more mobile than other groups, they were on hand in large numbers whenever and wherever workers were needed. This point will be further discussed in a later section. Here I wish to refer once again to Thomas Young, who describes a dance attended by Caribs, Creoles, and Moskito Indians, all joining together on apparently friendly terms (1847:32). This type of event would be most unlikely today.

Both Young (*ibid.*) and Bard note extreme physical heterogeneity within the Carib population at the middle of the nineteenth century. Bard says, "Most are pure Indians, not large, but muscular, with a ruddy skin, and long straight hair. . . . Another portion are very dark, with curly hair, and betraying unmistakably a large infusion of Negro blood. . ." (1855:317).

On the other hand, in 1899 Maudsley stated that the town of Livingston, Guatemala, was inhabited primarily by Negroes, called Caribs. "One can detect little trace of Indian blood by their appearance" (1899:155).

Today mixed marriages *do* take place, upon the Caribs' own admission, and according to my own observations, predominantly with Negroes. Outcast status contributes to the fact that the Caribs are ever acquiring more Negro genes in their total gene pool, for children resulting from mixed unions nearly always are raised as Caribs, being abandoned by their Negro parent. Nevertheless, the Caribs maintain as an ideal that they never intermarry with anyone outside their own group.

A study of blood types, carried out in Livingston in 1962, turned up one case positive for the Diego factor out of the sample of eighty-two unrelated adults with no *known* non-Carib admixture (Tejada, Gonzalez, and Sanchez 1965). This is a much lower frequency than has been reported for other groups of mixed African-Amerind ancestry (see Layrisse 1957), and would seem to support the view that this population is today of predominantly African origin.

Three

~~~~~~

THE ECONOMIC DEVELOPMENT OF
BLACK CARIB SOCIETY

~~~~~~

RISE OF THE BANANA INDUSTRY, 1870–1900

AS was shown in the preceding section, wage work was known among the Caribs throughout the whole of their residence in Central America, but it was only after the American Civil War, when schooners began visiting the Central American coast line to buy bananas and other fruits for transport to the United States, that almost all Carib men were able to find some type of wage labor comparatively close to their villages.

The earliest shipping from the area was from the Bay Islands, especially the island of Utila. Two Englishmen from Belize migrated to the islands about 1850 and began to make irregular shipments of coconuts, grapefruit, plantains, oranges, mangoes, bananas, and sarsaparilla to the United States. About 1860, they began to sail up and down the coast of Honduras buying fruit where they could from the natives. They were soon joined by others, and by the 1870's there were perhaps a dozen small independent companies, each owning only one or two schooners, in the waters. The natives of the area, including the Caribs, brought their fruit to the beaches; and the Caribs, with dugout canoes, carried the fruit to the schooners lying at anchor out from the shore. This purchase of small quantities of fruit from individual growers came to be known as *poquitero* buying, and became an important source of cash for the natives.

Poquitero buying existed all along the Central American coast between Costa Rica and Belize in the early days. Since the Caribs lived along most of this coast, it affected all of them, whether in Honduras or British Honduras. Many of them began planting bananas for sale, this being the responsibility of the men, while the women continued to plant the traditional crops. In 1887 W. T. Brigham, visiting Livingston, reported that bananas and plantains were its chief commercial crops, and that the town was then developing greater facilities for raising and shipping fruit. During that year bananas sold at fifty cents a bunch, one of the highest prices ever paid. Nevertheless, as a Guatemalan national export, bananas rated only fifth in 1889, following coffee, hides, rubber, and sugar (1887:38).

Because of the sporadic nature of the trade, the men were able to continue their fishing and other traditional occupations. They could, on the other hand, earn small amounts of cash without traveling too far away from home. The majority spent most of their time in the villages, perhaps making a few trips per year to British Honduras as *contrabandistas*. Perhaps the most important and far-reaching change during this period was the increased use of money. With the development of the banana trade, objects manufactured in the outer world became more readily available to the Caribs, and their wants increased in proportion. It was during this period that pottery making declined and finally died out. Their clothing, as described by

O. Henry in *Cabbages and Kings* (Porter 1904), was already of Western style, and they required goods to manufacture clothing, as well as implements such as machetes, iron fish-hooks and harpoon heads, cords for fishing lines and nets, and household furnishings, such as iron pots, dishes, chairs, and tables.

During the 1870's several small operators, most of them Italian-Americans from New Orleans, were carrying fruit from the Central American mainland to the United States. Between 1881 and 1889 five fruit companies registered in Belize for the purpose of transporting fruit from that colony to the United States. In 1885 a group of men, some of whom had already been in the trade, formed the Boston Fruit Company to bring fruit primarily from Jamaica to Boston. Minor C. Keith, who had been active in building railroads in Costa Rica, first planted bananas along his railroad line to increase the amount of freight carried, then began shipping bananas from Costa Rica to New York and New Orleans. In 1899 his Central American holdings were merged with the shipping facilities of the Boston Fruit Company, incorporated since 1890 with various subsidiary companies. With this merger the United Fruit Company was born.

DEPENDENCE UPON WAGE LABOR, 1900–1930

The turn of the century marked a change of far-reaching importance for the banana industry, as well as for the countries and peoples affected by its operations. The period of free competition was over and monopolistic practices and "big business" moved in to stay. As we shall see, the increased scope of the few remaining large companies at first raised the standard of living of the Caribs and other peoples employed by them. Eventually however, these groups became so dependent upon the banana trade that when it began to slacken and then disappeared almost entirely in certain areas, an unprecedented depression followed.

In 1904 Minor C. Keith contracted to build a railroad from Puerto Barrios to Guatemala City, a project which was completed in 1908. In 1906 the United Fruit Company obtained a concession of fifty thousand acres of land in the fertile Motagua Valley of Guatemala, where they began to establish banana farms. Livingston remained the center of *poquitero* buying operations in Guatemala, for the Río Dulce still provided the most efficient way of getting the bananas grown by private individuals down to the coast. The railway was most important to the company in transporting its own bananas to Puerto Barrios. [Caribs continued to be employed on the docks at Livingston and at Puerto Barrios, but the company imported laborers for its plantations from the West Indies, primarily from Jamaica.]

In 1911 the Cuyamel Fruit Company was formed, with headquarters at Puerto Cortes, Honduras. Its primary stockholders and managers were two men known as Hubbard and Zemurray, operators who had been buying fruit in the Honduras area for many years. This company continued to grow and develop, and became one of the most serious competitors of the United Fruit Company until it was purchased by the latter in 1929.

Meanwhile, the United Fruit Company obtained land in Honduras and started planting bananas there about 1912. Its center of operations was Tela, where the company built a wharf, a railroad terminal with branches extending into all of its banana plantations in the valleys of the Ulua and Chamelecon rivers, and a completely new town, with dwellings for workers of all classes, a power plant, a huge commissary, a bottling plant, and many other appendages which made New Tela almost self-sufficient in relation to the rest of the country.

The third large company which came into being during this period was the Standard Fruit Company, which was also a combination of several smaller operators who had been in the area for some time. The two primary concerns involved were the Vacarro Brothers and the Atlantic Fruit Company. The former had been buying fruit primarily in the Bay Islands and near La Ceiba and Trujillo, Honduras; the latter operated around Bluefields, Nicaragua. Thus, one or another of these large companies controlled virtually the entire wage-labor market of the north (Caribbean) coast of Honduras. Although at first glance it would seem that competition among the three would serve to keep prices of fruit and wages fairly high, in fact it was not so, for each operated only in its own territory and did not attempt to compete with the others in buying fruit. It is true that to a certain extent workers could move from area to area seeking the highest wages. Although this did occur, in times of labor shortage the companies, especially the United Fruit Company, recruited men from the West Indian islands, and the consequent flooding of the entire coast with excess labor kept the wages low.

This period saw the banana industry reach its highest development in Central America — particularly in Honduras, but also in Guatemala and British Honduras. Ships began to arrive on regular schedules to pick up fruit from the company plantations and from the *poquiteros*. At each of the port towns of Trujillo, La Ceiba, Tela, and Cortes (all in Honduras), and at Puerto Barrios, Guatemala, the companies employed a large number of men to unload cargo and then reload the ships with bananas. In the early days no records were kept of the number of men employed at each port, and it is impossible to provide exact figures to illustrate the importance of this form of labor. Nevertheless, old-time company officials have offered estimates, and it is also possible to draw inferences concerning the growth and decline of the trade from the number of stems exported from the two countries in selected years. These figures are shown in Table 1.

The companies found that Caribs worked very well as dock laborers. Indeed, they were employed in all phases of the transport process. However, Caribs were not used to any great extent on the plantations themselves. For this type of work the company found it necessary to import Negro labor from the

TABLE 1

EXPORTS IN BUNCHES OF BANANAS
FROM GUATEMALA AND HONDURAS, 1890–1955

Year	Guatemala	Honduras
1890	283,077	400,000
1900	121,234	4,772,417
1913	3,444,036	8,238,726
1929	6,545,695	28,221,463
1935	5,594,964	12,229,189
1951	5,264,831	9,666,433
1955	5,298,398	7,780,880

West Indian islands — particularly from Jamaica. The local Mestizos were extremely susceptible to malaria, endemic in the zone, whereas the Negroes were better able to withstand this disease. The Caribs, however, could not be persuaded to work inland, even though they shared the relative immunity to malaria shown by the West Indians.

Throughout this period the Caribs maintained, to a certain extent, their traditional horticultural activities. Though primarily the work of the women, horticulture was nearly impossible without the cooperation of males, who did the heavy work involved in tropical forest milpa cultivation. The men's work — cutting and clearing away of jungle and debris — had to be done each year. Then the women took over, while the men went back to their main occupation of fishing. Neither of these occupations took up the entire time of the men, however. Apparently from the time when the Black Caribs first emerged as a distinct ethnic group the men have found it possible to supplement these occupations with part-time or temporary forms of wage labor. The money earned through these jobs bought many items which early became necessities rather than luxuries. Still, the money received was not sufficient to support their families completely. Therefore they continued to fish and to help with cultivation, even though wage labor gradually came to be their dominant work. But fishing and cultivation were still thought of as essential, as they actually were

under the circumstances. For this reason, a Carib man had to
be in a position to return to his home from time to time when
his presence was demanded. Along the coast, travel by land is
still impossible in most places. Nearly all movement is by sea,
and the Caribs are famous for their skill in traveling great distances by dugout canoe. In former times most men and boys
over twelve years of age owned at least one canoe and could
handle it expertly. Thus, if a Carib could remain close to the
sea, which provided him with a familiar and inexpensive route
back home, he was willing to venture miles away in search of
work — but not inland, which was to him a far greater distance from his home. In addition, by remaining near the sea he
could always engage in his familiar occupation of fishing when
he was between jobs, and not only provide some food for himself and his dependents, but perhaps sell the surplus and make
a bit more money.

Another factor often presented to explain the Carib man's
refusal to work on plantations is that horticulture was considered "women's work" and beneath the dignity of a male. However, I believe this is probably less important than the former
necessity to remain near the sea, and thus near the home village. It is notable that during this period the Carib man had no
objection to cultivating his own bananas for sale, and that at
the present time there are some men who engage almost full
time in agriculture. The distinction between "women's work"
and "men's work" still exists, but it seems to be oriented primarily toward the crops grown, and not toward the cultivation
itself. The man willingly grows cacao, rice, beans, coconuts,
and bananas for sale, whereas he generally leaves the cultivation of the traditional garden crops — such as manioc, plantains, yams, and pineapples — to his womenfolk.

During this second period, then, the Carib man gradually
devoted more and more of his time to absentee wage labor, but
he did keep himself in a position to return home frequently.
Actually, there was a good deal of work available fairly close
to the Carib villages. Many of the men were able to return

home each night. But, at the same time, the culture as a whole was moving away from a subsistence economy based on horticulture and fishing supplemented by wage labor, to an economy based upon wage labor, with horticulture and fishing serving merely as subsidiary activities. And this new economy was dependent almost entirely upon employment in the banana industry. This must be kept in mind as the primary factor leading to the next period, which I have termed "depression."

DEPRESSION, 1930 TO THE PRESENT

The events of the decade following 1930 led to the virtual collapse of the system to which the Caribs had become adapted. Let us follow the events which occurred in Livingston, Guatemala, as one example of what happened during that decade.

This town was the headquarters of the United Fruit Company operations in Guatemala. Livingston's harbor is shallow, and large vessels cannot come in close to shore, but it is at the mouth of the Río Dulce, a navigable river emptying into Lake Izabal, the largest lake in Guatemala. Before the railroad was built between Guatemala City and Puerto Barrios, bananas were brought to the coast on barges, through the lake and down the Río Dulce, and loaded on company ships which stood out in the bay. A long-time company official, formerly port superintendent in Livingston, informed me that in the 1930's virtually all available labor in this area was Carib. A few Ladinos were employed for office work, but Caribs worked on the launches and barges up and down the river, and loaded bananas in the bay. According to several informants, as many as twenty thousand to thirty thousand stems were loaded per week from the Livingston area. Five ships arrived every week, anchoring about one or two miles out from shore. Each carried a cargo of about ten thousand stems. After loading perhaps five thousand to seven thousand stems at Livingston, the ships continued up the coast into British Honduras, stopping at Punta Gorda, Monkey River, Seine Bight, All Pines, Mullins River, Stann Creek, Sittee River, and Belize, picking up more bananas at each point. Among these towns Punta Gorda, Seine Bight, and Stann Creek are composed entirely, or mostly, of Caribs. The other two Carib towns in British Honduras — Barranco and Hopkins — are close enough to others of these towns listed as steamer calls so that men might easily go there to work and return home the next day.

Although the railroad connecting Puerto Barrios to Guatemala City was completed in 1908, so long as the company was still buying bananas directly from individual producers, the only way to transport them to the coast was via the Río Dulce and Livingston. Thus, even though the main headquarters of the company was moved to Puerto Barrios after completion of the railroad, Livingston continued to be important up to about 1939.

[In that year the company stopped purchasing bananas and moved all of its operations to Puerto Barrios. In the words of an elderly Carib informant, "That killed this place."]Many reasons are given by the general populace as to why this happened. The most usual is that two diseases, called Panama disease and sigatoka, ruined the bananas and thus the business. Undoubtedly, this was an important point, but other testimony suggests additional factors. Sigatoka can be controlled by spraying, but, for a number of involved reasons, it was difficult to induce the private owners to spray. The quality of their bananas steadily decreased, while concurrently the banana industry and, more importantly, consumers became more sophisticated. Consumers in the early days would buy any kind of banana, but later they demanded increased size and quality, rejecting what did not meet their standards. In short, it became more profitable for the company to bring to its United States markets only standardized products which could more successfully and profitably be raised on its own plantations.

The effect of Panama disease, with a still unknown etiology, has been more serious. Lands affected by this scourge are rendered virtually worthless for growing bananas. In the past twenty-five years the company has abandoned thousands of acres of land in the Black Carib area for this reason. Most notable in connection with the present account have been the complete evacuation of the port of Castilla near Trujillo, Honduras, and the virtual cessation of all company operations in the colony of British Honduras.

The picture can also be reconstructed by examining events during the 1930's which affected the fruit industry as a whole. In 1930, as a result in part of the world economic depression and in part of the fact that Panama disease was making huge inroads in the plantations, the company found it necessary to economize on a grand scale. Therefore, all divisions were ordered to cut the labor force drastically. It has been reported that the United Fruit Company weeded out one worker in every four (Kepner 1936:144). *La Tribuna*, a newspaper of San José, Costa Rica, reported in 1930 that two thousand laborers had been thrown out of work on the Atlantic coast of Costa Rica alone. The same situation seems to have held for the other countries as well. One system was to cut the total labor force and require each man to work longer and harder at his particular job for the same wages. However, after cutting down on the total number and stepping up the requirements for each worker, the company also cut wages by 20 per cent in 1931 (Kepner and Soothill 1935:137). Discontent founded on real hardship grew rapidly as a result of these changes, and in 1932 the dock workers at Tela, Honduras, most of whom were Caribs, struck for higher wages. The strike was put down by the company's private police force and with the aid of the government. Nevertheless, other strikes were held periodically in all parts of the territory, and it has been suggested that the number of revolutionary outbreaks in Honduras during the early 1930's was also influenced by the general unemployment and discontent (Kepner 1936:134, 197).

The Caribs, whose history seems to show a series of involvements in political events, became concerned with a plot to overthrow the Honduran government in 1937. The principal group involved was from the village of San Juan, near the trouble spot of Tela. The plot was discovered, and a number of Carib men were executed in the village streets as an example. Others managed to escape this fate by fleeing to British Honduras.

By 1940 the Caribs, who had come to depend on wage labor and money as the basis of their economy, found the old system based on fishing and horticulture not only inadequate for their needs but also beneath their dignity. Yet by 1940 there were few jobs to be found, in Guatemala, in the colony of British Honduras, or yet in Honduras — the area over which they and their ancestors had traveled to find jobs in the past.

From the very earliest days of the settlement and expansion period to the present time, Caribs have been traveling from home to secure wage labor. However, it is apparent that the behavior patterns of the men engaged in this activity have been far from uniform. They have varied according to the amount of work available at different times and places, the needs of the Caribs for cash, and, lately, the policies of the fruit companies for whom so many of them work and the labor laws of the countries within which they reside. Up until 1900 men who wished to earn a small amount of cash generally could do so fairly close to their home villages by contracting to transport bananas from the shore to waiting offshore steamers. They could also journey to British Honduras to work in mahogany and logwood cutting. Evidence both from travelers' accounts and from elderly informants indicates that in these early days those who migrated long distances for several months or years at a time were primarily young unmarried men. Such men were especially in need of cash to help them accumulate goods of the proper kind and amount to contract a marriage. After marriage a man tended to remain nearer home and engage in traditional economic activities, such as fishing, hunting, and clearing fields.

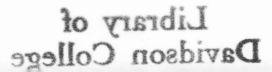

Air view of Carib village near Trujillo, Honduras,
showing settlement pattern, 1956.

Three Carib young men, 1956.

Woman making a cassava grater. The grater itself and her clothing illustrate something of the "traditional culture."

Carib children on the beach. Note canoes in the background.

This type of migratory wage labor, which we may term "temporary, nonseasonal," is found rather frequently in the world, and it does not seem to alter the existing native social structure to any great extent (see Chapter VI).

Another important factor leading to depression was the shift in attitude, and consequently in the employment system, of the fruit companies. In the early years workers were hired more or less on the spot as they were needed. A man worked when he wished and when he had time. As the industry grew larger and more complex, requiring standardized procedures, regular shipping schedules, and the like, definite labor policies also came into being. These policies were later complicated by the development of labor laws in the countries involved.

The practice of moving freely from country to country in the search for work became more difficult when the different nations passed laws prohibiting the employment of foreigners. In Guatemala, this occurred in 1914. Today in that country there is a small quota of foreigners which any firm may employ. It is also necessary for the job seeker (whether a citizen or an immigrant) to secure a *cedula*, or official identification card, before being employed. It was reported to me in Puerto Barrios that these could be secured illegally by paying bribes to officials to short-circuit the regular procedure. This practice was known locally by the term "*submarino*."

In 1931 the government passed a minimum age law stipulating that a man must be at least eighteen years of age before going to work on the docks. Before that, male children between eleven and fifteen were employed as water carriers, and then as they matured they might move into the stevedore class.

After about 1930 workers were required to be registered and were expected to present themselves for work whenever the company demanded them. This in itself necessitated a change in the orientation of the Carib toward his work. He had become accustomed to working intermittently, according to his own needs for money, and had always been free to return to his village to help his womenfolk, fish, participate in religious ceremonies, build houses, and so forth. Now he found that he was likely to lose his opportunity to work at all if he did not conform to the schedules required by the company.

At first the companies made a policy of carrying many more men on their employment rolls than were needed at any one time. The men worked in gangs, and each gang might be called on only two or three days per week, thus permitting some free time for domestic pursuits. However, since 1930 the companies have gradually decreased the total number of men employed and expected these men to work more steadily.

At the time of my field work I found that the United Fruit Company employed about 850 men on the docks at Puerto Barrios, Guatemala, and a subsidiary company, ostensibly run by Guatemalans, employed about 575 more. A new port, Matias de Gálvez, a few miles from Puerto Barrios, was just beginning to hire dock workers in 1956, and within a decade had become an important employment opportunity in the area. In addition, there has developed a sawmill in Barrios, as well as one in Livingston itself, which employ perhaps two hundred men between them.

In 1956 the United Fruit Company employed about 500 men at the Honduran port of Cortes, and a local steamship company had an employee roll of about 650, of which some 400 to 500 were actually working on board ships at any one time, the rest being in between jobs. At Tela, also in Honduras, the United Fruit Company reported 240 men employed as dock workers, although only about half of these worked at any one time. In La Ceiba, Honduras, the Standard Fruit Company employed about 400 men on the wharf, and even provided transportation for the men from their villages, which were about 15 or 20 kilometers from the port.

In British Honduras there were few opportunities for dock work, for the reasons outlined above, but other enterprises employed Caribs up and down the coast. At Stann Creek there was a grapefruit farm, the produce of which was canned and exported locally. About fifteen hundred persons were employed in these combined operations — many of them women, especially in the cannery. Some wood cutting was done on an individual contract basis, both in the colony and in Guatemala, and a sawmill near the town of Mango Creek employed many Caribs from Seine Bight, Hopkins, and Punta Gorda — all villages in British Honduras. The managers informed me in 1956 that about three hundred men were on their rolls. In this and the other cases mentioned above, these figures refer to the total numbers of men employed. It is impossible to get exact figures on numbers of Caribs represented. It should be realized that there were also non-Caribs competing for these positions, and this too was a factor of great concern to the Carib men interviewed. However, throughout the area surveyed for this study, it was pointed out that these particular types of work were generally those greatly sought by Caribs. Other types of employment — such as upon the banana farms in Honduras — were not so popular with Caribs as with Mestizos and Negroes. Therefore, these figures are presented more to show the *opportunities* for employment available to Caribs, given their peculiar preferences, at the time of the study. Possibly from two-thirds to three-fourths of these labor forces were actually made up of Caribs, but I have no way of proving this point.

Although the dock work was more or less constant through the year, there were some seasonal variations. However, the other types of employment mentioned above were even more subject to the vagaries of the season. Thus, the grapefruit industry employed large numbers of people only from September through April of each year, retaining just a skeleton force the rest of the time. The sawmills had their heaviest work from November or December through June, while the wood cutting was done during the rainy season, from June through December, when the rivers were high enough to float the cut logs down to the coast. The seasonal nature of much of the work caused some moving about from place to place, and also permitted some periods when the man could return home.

⌐ As the Carib economy came more and more to depend upon wage labor, however, and as some of the operations were streamlined by the companies involved, certain changes in the migration patterns developed. In many cases, these changes have caused a man to move away from his home village and even to cut many ties with his society.⌐In each of the main ports (Barrios, Cortes, Tela, La Ceiba) there have grown up Carib communities within the larger community where many of the workers live with or without their families. Some of these maintain a house in their home village as well, returning there only occasionally for special occasions, but in many cases these Caribs have become full-time residents of the towns, and in the process have changed their entire pattern of living. They become acculturated rapidly — their children are better educated, acquire new ideals and goals, and begin to look down on the village Carib. Eventually they give up their native speech, change their pattern of dress, and try to "pass" as non-Carib Negroes.

Four

BLACK CARIB DOMESTIC LIFE

I shall now describe the everyday functioning of the domestic unit in Carib society — the household. The household is defined here as the group of people who live under one roof, who eat and sleep together, and who cooperate daily for the common benefit of all. A household may derive nearly all its financial support from nonmembers, but economic cooperation of some sort is characteristic of the group.

Before describing the typical structure of the various household groups among the Black Caribs, it is necessary to give some idea of how all such units must function — that is, what things need to be done and how the culture dictates that they shall be carried out.

As in all societies, division of labor is based upon sex, as well as upon age. However, in recent years certain changes have occurred in the patterns of behavior formerly typical of Carib society, especially in the differential activities of men and women. The following account first sets forth the traditional patterns, based entirely upon informants' statements, then more completely describes present-day customs.

TRADITIONAL PATTERNS OF BEHAVIOR

It was traditional in Black Carib culture for the women to be the primary agricultural producers. Men contributed in this sphere by clearing and burning the land in preparation for planting, but after that the women took over and completed the cycle of cultivation and harvesting. A woman's responsibility did not end with the harvest — she also processed the foods produced and converted them into edible form. For bitter manioc, this involved the laborious task of expressing the poisonous acid, and the manufacture of *areba*, or cassava bread, the main staple. Rice was dried in the sun, pounded in a mortar to remove the hulls, and cooked each day. The women grew plantains, which they carried in from the fields and, most typically, pounded into a paste called *hudutu baruru* (pounded plantain), a favorite food in coastal Central America as well as throughout the Caribbean. Women gathered crabs and other shellfish, such as snails and certain varieties of shrimp, to contribute to the household food supply. They also processed fish brought in by the men, drying and salting them for the household and for sale.

The woman had the responsibility of raising children — caring for their needs, disciplining them, and teaching them morals and everyday behavior — up to the age of about ten, when the men took over much of the training of the boys, the girls remaining under the supervision of their mothers until marriage.

Women also washed clothing, cleaned the house and the yard, and often had a small vegetable garden near the house in addition to the fields, which were in the "bush," from fifteen minutes' up to an hour's walk away.

Duties of the men included fishing and to some extent hunt-

ing, although the latter has never been extremely important.
Men supplied their own wives and children with fish, but also
were obliged to give a share to certain relatives, primarily to
their mothers-in-law, but also to their own parents and sisters.
They spent a great deal of time making and mending their fishing equipment, which included hooks and lines, basketry
traps, circular cast nets, seines, harpoons, and bows and ar-
rows. A recent article by Richard Price describes the historical
development of Caribbean fishing technology. He suggests that
"the unusual socioeconomic role [of slave fishermen] permitted a particularly smooth transformation to a life as free fishermen" (1966:1363). It is interesting to note that the Black
Caribs were never an enslaved group, yet their fishing technology incorporated most, if not all, of the elements described by
Price — presumably because they had the same pool of elements from which to draw as did other West Indians of the
Lesser Antilles, and because those tools and techniques
adopted increased the effectiveness of their efforts. In regard to
the sociological concomitants suggested, but not described, by
Price, it would be interesting to compare more rigorously the
Black Caribs with other present-day fishing groups to determine which elements can be traced back to the socioeconomic
role of the slave fisherman, and which are simply related to the
fishing economy per se. In the case of the Black Caribs, it
seems to me that this same fishing economy permitted a relatively smooth transition to life as wage laborers, as we shall see
below.

In addition to the above tasks, men also manufactured all
basketry items used by the household, including equipment for
processing manioc, containers for storing food and clothing,
and baskets for carrying produce in from the fields. They also
did woodwork, making their dugout canoes, mortars and pestles, furniture for the houses, various wooden bowls and plates
for household use, and cassava graters (although to the
women fell the task of inserting the small pieces of flint into
the boards shaped by the men).

Men built the houses, generally enlisting the aid of relatives and neighbors, who often formed themselves into cooperative groups to help each other in this task. They kept the house in repair, replacing the thatched roofs or rotten boards when necessary.

It is difficult to determine just how much the father assisted in the care of the children in the early days, but according to the tales told by some informants he played an important part in educating his male children after the age of about ten. From this point on he took the boy fishing with him, teaching him how to manage a canoe, how to cast a net, where the fish were apt to be found, and so forth. He was also responsible for teaching the boys how to manufacture those items ordinarily made by men.

The couvade was practiced, suggesting that in former days a strong bond existed between father and child, as well as between mother and child. This is no longer so important in the present-day culture, although older informants still remember most of its elements, and a few of the younger men claim that they carry out some of its obligations. The belief was that the child received its body and blood from the mother and its soul from the father. Therefore, at the time of birth and for forty days after, the activities of the father had an important direct bearing on the welfare of the newborn child. The father was not supposed to do any heavy labor, especially anything which involved the use of a cutting instrument. He was not to kill any animal or reptile, particularly not a snake, and he had to avoid eating certain foods. Most important, he must not have sexual intercourse with any other woman. This last item is one of the few elements whose consequences modern informants still fear.[1]

[1] Robert and Ruth Munroe have recently completed a study of the couvade among the Black Caribs of British Honduras, and they concluded that the institution persists more strongly than I supposed. Since they were particularly concerned with such matters, and I was not, it may be that they uncovered information which eluded me. On the other

When the children were ready for marriage, both parents had a great influence upon the selection of a proper mate, although the young people themselves had some choice in the matter. It is clear that the parents acted either to approve or to veto the choices the children made for themselves.

The Caribs insist that formerly polygyny was common, though not universal, among them. The households as described were generally uxorilocal, in which the woman continued to live in her home village, the man visiting his several wives in turn. On the other hand, some Caribs report that formerly a man might keep several wives in the same household, all cooperating with the domestic chores.

Young (1847:123) gives us still a different description. According to him, each wife had equal, but separate status. The man built each a house and cleared a "plantation" for her. After this, each wife was responsible to maintain herself and her children from the produce of her garden. Bard (1855:318) adds that the huts of several wives were built contiguously.

Obviously, it is difficult to judge just what the system was in earlier times, though it is probably safe to assume that polygyny was acceptable and common. It is possible that all of these alternatives and more existed, depending upon the age, position, and wealth of the man. It should be remembered that at the time of Young's visit, Black Carib society was in a formative state, beginning to adapt itself to an increasing dependence upon migrant wage labor.

It appears that the individual household or family group was never autonomous in matters concerning the supernatural. Generally segments of a larger kinship group cooperated in making offerings to various ancestral spirits, calling in members from towns and villages up and down the coast when a

---

hand, the situation in Livingston, which is a relatively sophisticated town, may in fact be different. I am unable to reconcile this apparent difference in our interpretations at the present time (see Munroe *et al.* 1965).

ritual was to be performed. Both men and women had important duties to perform in these. The women were responsible
for preparing the food offerings in a way which would be acceptable to the ancestors. On the other hand, the men made
the baskets into which the food was placed, and arranged for
drummers (who were and still are males). The *buwiye*, or sha-
man, was in charge of the proceedings, and this office, which
could be filled by either a man or a woman, was in most cases
held by a man. The presence of both sexes was considered to
be necessary for the proper fulfillment of the rite, and both
sexes participated in the singing and dancing. It is interesting,
however, to note that it was far more often women than men
who danced on and on into a state of spirit possession.

MODERN PATTERNS OF BEHAVIOR

We have seen that the modern economic system of the
Black Carib has arisen during the past two generations. I will
now attempt to show the primary social consequences of the
new system by comparing the roles played by men and women
in the domestic unit today with those of earlier times, which I
discussed previously.

As before, women are in charge of raising the childen. This
responsibility has increased today with the more frequent temporary or permanent absence of a husband-father, who formerly helped with some aspects of the child's socialization.
Actually, as we shall see, institutions have developed which
enable the mother to distribute these duties among certain of
her kinsmen or even to individuals outside the Carib ethnic
group itself. In spite of these, the mother still has the ultimate
responsibility for each child.

The woman also plays an important part in the economic
system — particularly in horticulture for subsistence purposes.
Her activities in regard to planting, cultivating, and harvesting
remain similar to those of the woman under earlier conditions,
but her burden has been increased by the fact that she has less

help from the man than in earlier times. The clearing and burning of the forest, formerly carried out by the husband in the family, is now often left to the woman to take care of as best she can. In some cases she attempts to do it herself, but if the work is too heavy she calls upon her sons, brothers, or perhaps mother's brothers, or she may hire a man to come in and do it for her. That this lack of help has been typical for some time is reflected in the words of a song sung by the Black Caribs, which informants believe is at least fifty years old. The song tells of a mockingbird singing, signaling the approach of the dry season when clearing and burning should be done. A woman, hearing the bird, laments that she is not a man, not strong like a man, yet she must go to the fields and somehow get them ready for planting.[2] It is, then, the woman's responsibility to provide food for herself and her children, and for her husband if he happens to be living with her.

Most women today find it impossible to support themselves and their children without the addition of cash income from some source. If possible, this is secured from a man — a husband, the fathers of her children, an adult brother, or an adult son. If there are no men to whom she can turn, she may find it necessary to secure a wage income of some sort for herself. She might market surplus produce from her fields, act as a middleman in the distribution of fish, take in laundry of non-Caribs (this is possible, of course, only in the larger towns where other ethnic groups are also living), raise chickens or a cow and sell the eggs or milk, or leave the village to secure employment as a domestic worker in a middle- or upper-class white household. If she goes away, she seldom can take her children with her, but rather leaves them, usually with her mother or another female relative on her mother's side.

An adult woman must form cooperative ties, then, with

[2] 'rita ti'yayo gu'rasuwe i'rumu
'rita ti-yayo gu'rasuwe i'rumune
ta'gambaguwa gu'waguda ya-dina
'saguru me'yeri 'nanine pi'fanyo
'saguru me'yeri 'nanine a ma'rawa.

both men and women in order to maintain herself and her children. Even if the woman remains in the village and is able to secure some cash income through her own activities or by rights due her through her relationship with some male, she finds that it is an almost impossible task to live alone with her children and still manage to raise them properly while carrying on her economic activities at the same time. This is true because she must be absent from the house itself for a considerable portion of her time, regardless of what she does. I believe that the patterned series of household structures described below can be interpreted as an adaptive response to this situation, as can the structure of the interrelationships among members of the household group.

The position of the mother's mother is a highly important one, for she is often the person who actually cares for an individual during the first early years. As a woman grows older, she spends less time in activities directly related to earning a living, leaving this to her daughters and adult sons, who in turn are responsible for supporting her. The system can be regarded as a mechanism providing not only for the care of young children, but also for the aged, since old women, especially, would otherwise often be left unaided. Although in later life many couples settle down and marry according to Western custom, this does not happen in all cases. In addition, the total number of old women is far greater than that of old men. In Livingston, at the time of this study, there were forty-nine men over the age of sixty, and ninety women in the same age bracket (see Table 2). Even if a woman is actually married to a man at the time of his death, it is her own maternal relatives or her own children who are responsible for her later — *not* the family of her husband.

Another institution which functions to assist the woman left alone with young children is that of child loaning. This will be discussed further in connection with the structure of the household group; however, I wish to emphasize that loaning is different from the practice of leaving a child with relatives of the mother during her temporary absence. In true loaning no kinship bond need exist between the child and the family with which he goes to live, even though in many cases he may be treated as though he were a relative by the family. He may be addressed with kinship terms by other members of the household group, but he has no obligation to the family ancestors of this household, nor may he claim inheritance rights. The arrangement seems to be entirely economic. Many times a family will accept a fairly young child before he (or she) becomes an economic asset, with the understanding that he will remain with them when his labor may be of real value. Even young children help with household tasks, doing such things as carrying water, running errands, sweeping the house and compound, carrying dirt to repair floors, disposing of garbage, and the like. Children of three or four may carry out many of these activities. Thus, if a mother has several very young children and a neighboring household has none, both parties may find it advantageous to set up a loaning arrangement. The child does not lose contact with his own mother and her family during this time, however. He usually sees them every day unless the harboring family lives a great distance away, and in any case he makes fairly regular visits back home. During the time that he lives with them, the host family provides food, clothing, and shelter, and is responsible for the child's behavior.

Still another practice is that of sending young children, usually boys, to live with middle- or upper-class white families. White informants in British Honduras and also in Honduras told me that Caribs often come into town and merely deposit their young sons of about ten years or so with any family they can get to accept him. From the point of view of the Caribs, this arrangement has several advantages. First, the financial burden of caring for this child is removed from his kin, and second, the child learns something of non-Carib patterns of culture, including a new language — either Spanish or English. The harboring family generally sees to it that the boy receives schooling of some sort, and when he finally grows up they assist him in finding a job. He pays for these services by helping about the house and garden, gradually taking on more and more duties as he grows older.

One of the obvious disadvantages of this type of arrangement from the point of view of Carib culture is that these children grow up with little knowledge of the traditional Carib ways of doing things. Although they may visit their home villages and receive visits from their mothers, still their values and orientation are definitely altered and channeled toward those of Western civilization. When these children grow up they may return to the village to find a wife and may even settle there intermittently, living according to the patterns set forth earlier, or they may remain permanently in the larger towns and leave Carib culture behind them. I would judge that the latter process is more frequent at the present time. In a sense then, this mechanism works against the interests of the ethnic society, for it tends to aggravate the situation which removes men from the villages for other reasons as they approach manhood. The result is a continual permanent loss of men which exceeds that of women.

In summary, the activities of the woman within the household group include not only all the duties she formerly had under the traditional system — including the production and preparation of food, care of young children, manufacture and care of clothing, and care of the household and compound — but also an additional burden brought about by the draining of men from the system, either temporarily or permanently.

Table 2 shows the sex ratio at each decade of life in the town of Livingston at the time of this study. It may be seen from the table that in each decade, except that of persons aged two to ten, there is a marked excess of females over males, the imbalance being almost even through the decades of adulthood rather than becoming gradually felt toward old age. It should be noted that persons were only listed as being "absent" if their absence was considered to be temporary and if they were expected to return. Although there were cases in which a

TABLE 2

Sex Ratios by Decade of Life Among Caribs in Livingston, Guatemala, 1956

Age	MALES			FEMALES			Excess of Females over Males	Sex Ratio
	Present	Absent	Total	Present	Absent	Total		
0–1	39	2	41	55	0	55	14	.7454
2–10	174	8	182	171	10	181	–1	1.0055
11–20	109	30	139	188	21	209	70	.6651
21–30	72	36	108	115	23	138	30	.7826
31–40	72	21	93	113	21	134	41	.6940
41–50	59	18	77	102	9	111	34	.6937
51–60	49	24	73	77	5	82	9	.8902
61–70	27	3	30	55	0	55	25	.5455
Over 70	19	0	19	35	0	35	16	.5426
Total	620	142	762	911	89	1,000	238	—

person had been absent for twenty-five years on a "visit," these are actually rare.

The general pattern of these figures shows a gradually rising number of men absent during the most productive years of life — from twenty-one to fifty — followed by a tapering off again as they come home to settle down in the village. The figures for the decade eleven to twenty, which show a disproportionately large number of absent males, is probably attributable to the custom discussed above of placing young boys with white families in other towns. The fact that in all decades *except* two to ten there is a significant excess of females over males is also evidence of the fact that more men leave the village permanently than do women. The excess at all ages is too great to be explained merely by the fact that more females than males are born. The period from January, 1956, through April, 1957, shows a total of 164 male births as compared with 180 female births. These figures, when compared with the total number of children from zero to one years of age give an indication of the extremely high infant mortality rate.

If we now examine the role played by the adult male in the modern social organization, we shall find a number of more far-reaching changes which can be directly related to the shift to dependence upon wage labor. As we have seen, the modern Carib husband is primarily concerned with earning money. He may be considered to have moved out of the confines of the purely domestic economy which is now carried on primarily by the women. From the time he is old enough to get a job, he is looked to by various females for help in terms of cash, whereas under the old system it was his actual labor which was required in certain domestic duties. However, it cannot be emphasized too strongly that the man in his role as brother or son, though also looked to as a source of cash by the women, *is* called upon to help with domestic duties. I shall now analyze his relationship to the various women with whom he comes into contact and to whom he is related, either consanguineally or affinally, at various times of his life.

As soon as he is eighteen years old and may take out his legal work permit, it is considered proper for a man to find a wage-paying job. In order to do this he almost inevitably must leave his home village, unless it happens to be one of the port towns. He may live close enough to some source of labor so that he may return home frequently, or he may have to go some distance. If he works far from home he may return at intervals of several months or a year; in time he may settle permanently away from his natal village, depending on whether he finds a relatively secure and stable position which will allow him to settle down for a time. If he does not, he will probably continue to consider his natal village "home" and endeavor to return for important holidays and for visits.

If he is the youngest child, his parents will be especially loath to have him leave permanently and will attempt to keep the ties as strong as possible. This is particularly true of his mother, if she has not settled permanently with a man in a marital relationship of some kind. She will depend heavily upon her children as she grows older — upon her daughters for actual household assistance, and upon her sons, especially the youngest, for money. There are, however, few institutionalized mechanisms for retaining the loyalties of sons; for example, there is no promise of inheritance of great wealth or property, except perhaps a house and the lot upon which it stands.

The strength of the ancestor cult does tend to tie the son to his natal home, since he is required to participate in all rituals for his dead ancestors, and may be called home from work to do so. Now, however, such rites are becoming increasingly infrequent, and in any case the younger people are often highly skeptical. There is an attempt to uphold this tie through inculcation of a sense of moral responsibility in the young child. Many stories and myths emphasize that the "good" Carib man remains faithful to his mother, providing for her in her old age, and also that he has certain obligations to assist his otherwise helpless sisters. However, this is not always sufficient to prevent men from breaking all ties, even when their mothers may be in dire need. It does seem to hold men to their natal groups during the younger adult years, but as they grow older, if they succeed in becoming economically secure, their obligations and loyalties to their wife or wives *may* begin to supersede those to their mothers and sisters.

For example, in Livingston I observed a case in which an old woman, after several periods of illness, was expected to die shortly. Her living relatives included one sister, a brother, and three adult sons. She was being cared for primarily by her sister, one daughter-in-law, and her second son (not the husband of the daughter-in-law). A different house in the same compound was occupied by her brother, his daughter, and the daughter's children. One of the old woman's sons lived in the town of Puerto Cortes in Honduras, three-days' distance by canoe. This son had not been in contact with his mother for some time, but when she became ill the relatives summoned him to help care for his mother and to be present in case of death. They wrote to him several times, but he never answered the letters or telegrams. Personal messages sent through travelers also failed to elicit a response. Although his brothers and other relatives were shocked by this behavior, there was nothing they could do about it, and eventually they gave up. They did not forget the incident, however, and they predicted much future misfortune for him as a result of his neglect.

Another example of how control must be exercised to keep an employed adult son attached to his natal family is the case of José M. This young man, aged twenty, was living in his mother's house with her, his two adult sisters, and the three small children of the latter. He also had a wife and two young children who were living with her mother in another part of town. He had a job in Puerto Barrios with the United Fruit Company, and managed to get back to Livingston once every two or three weeks. He was expected to contribute to the support of his wife and their children, but the bulk of his wages was supposed to go to his mother. However, he had to be

"watched," for he often was lax in delivering cash to these dependents in Livingston. Each payday it was necessary for his
older sister to go to Puerto Barrios to confront him and collect
the cash for both her mother and his wife. At this time his wife
was pregnant, and her movements were thus restricted, but at
other times she would alternate with his sister in making the
trip to collect from him. His wife, however, apparently had
less difficulty in getting him to transmit money to her for support of herself and their two children. This he did willingly,
for they were still formally attached to one another. But his
sister was required to remind him of his duties to his mother.
That she was able to secure this money from him without difficulty by confronting him exemplifies the attitude and behavior
which exists between brother and sister, and especially reflects
the fact that age differences are extremely important among
siblings in regard to authority patterns. The sister in question
was the oldest child in the family, and his senior by ten
years. A younger sister would have had more difficulty in securing the money, and she would have gone about it by appealing to him as her big brother who should take care of his
younger sister. An older brother could have exerted the authority of his seniority; a younger brother would have had the
least influence of all.

As a young man moves into the category termed "adult" in
Carib society, he is likely to spend from five to ten years living
in the house of his mother or another of his maternal kin. During this time he has a particular role to play as "adult son," or
"adult brother," or both. He is increasingly looked to for
money and, to a lesser extent, for help about the household itself, such as repairing the house, cleaning the yard, building
chicken coops, and the like. Actually, his duties in these two
areas may be seen as merely a continuation of his childhood
responsibilities. Children begin helping about the house from
the age of about three, and as they grow older they are given
heavier and more responsible tasks to perform. An adolescent
boy may be required to contribute to the monetary income of

the family by shining shoes, by selling bread or sweets which his mother or sister makes, or by providing food in the form of fish. When he reaches adulthood — that is, when he secures a relatively steady wage-paying job — the emphasis switches from household help to monetary assistance, although it should be remembered that he has contributed in both of these areas for some time beforehand. In the intervals when he has no job, he will spend more time about the house and in fishing.

During this period of his life the man has little authority within the household group, since his mother remains the head of the house and it is she who makes decisions. When the man's sisters begin to have children, he acquires a definite authority role in regard to the sister's children. He disciplines them, teaches them manners and morals, plays with them, and, in contributing to the support of the household, also helps provide for them. Interestingly enough, the children often address him as "Papa." If the man has younger sisters, he will also have held an authoritative role in relation to them throughout life, and when they become adult he will be influential in controlling their behavior, especially in regard to sex. It is often noted by male informants that if you want to "make time" with a girl, it is a good idea to get on the good side of her older brothers, who may be living in the same household. In the absence of an older man who plays the role of "father" to a younger sister (and this may be either her genitor, a more recent husband of her mother, or her mother's brother), her own brother may control her behavior by keeping her in the house at night. If she should become pregnant, her brother may attempt to locate the father of her child and, in the event that he does not willingly recognize the child, try to force him to do so.

During this period of his life a young man will probably contract one or more marriages with young women in his own or a neighboring village, but the residence of each partner remains as it had been before the marriage. The young husband will visit his wife's home freely during the day and the night, eating an occasional meal there, helping out with household repairs, and giving her money from time to time. If there are no children, his contribution of money may be very slight at first, only enough to clothe his wife and buy a few luxuries now and then. If he goes fishing he will contribute a few fish to her household, or if he works for a fruit company he may now and then bring a few hands of green rejected bananas to the house. When children arrive, his obligation becomes greater, for he is expected to contribute substantially to their support, and this, of course, requires money. His relationship to his children is an affectionate one — he visits them often, bringing little gifts of toys or pennies as they grow older, but he seldom has much to do with their discipline. Informants often said that fathers were no good as disciplinarians, they indulged their children too much, and that if the mother really needed help she called in one of her male maternal kinsmen.

By the time a young man reaches the age of thirty or so, his life may take on a radically different form, in that he may have achieved a fairly high-paying job. Now he may find it possible and desirable, for purposes of increasing his prestige, to build a house in which to place his wife and children. By this time he will probably have had a series of alliances with different women, and he will usually have some children. He may set up housekeeping with his current favorite, or he may still feel loyalty for his first wife, if she does not have another husband. Whether or not the ties remain in any such relationship seems to depend on a number of things, some of which will be discussed in the section on marriage. Men who move around more in getting jobs delay longer in setting up a household, and some never do so, instead returning in later life to settle once again in the house or compound of their maternal relatives, by this time usually that of their own sisters and brothers.

Even if he does set up a house for one of his wives, he usually does not at this time marry her according to Western tradition. He may live with her for a while, but he may also maintain alliances with other women who remain with their own mothers, and he may live alternately with each or continue to live in his own mother's house.

In some cases a young couple of about thirty will enter into Western-type marriage, but invariably this is a couple who intend to leave the village and settle elsewhere near the husband's work. Usually the man holds some sort of white-collar or skilled-labor position in a non-Carib community. These marriages are no more stable than those I have termed "ethnic" marriages.[3] Legal divorce is almost nonexistent; if the marriages sanctioned by the state and the church break up, neither party can contract another of the same type — a fact which does not prevent each from living with other persons without the benefit of formal ties.

We must now consider the role played by the man who lives in a household as a husband and father. In this position he holds more responsibility and authority than he had when living with his mother. He becomes the head of the house and makes decisions concerning the household members. His authority over his wife is maintained by the fact that he may at any time leave her, and in a society where women considerably outnumber the men, and in which a woman needs the monetary assistance of a man, she will go to great lengths to hold him. It is well recognized by both that while he may usually find another woman with ease, she may have difficulty finding another man who will be willing to support her and her children. If he leaves, her financial burden will be considerable, and she will be forced to find some other means of obtaining money. As described before, this will almost always entail living with some other adult kin in order to carry out successfully all the necessary domestic duties. Cooperative ties with her mother, her mother's mother, a sister, a maternal aunt, a brother, or a mother's brother are the most common. Since these may have other obligations, and since marriage is most

[3] See below, Chapter V.

prestigious, such alternatives, though common, are not preferred. Therefore, very often a man living with a woman becomes a sort of despot; he may even beat her from time to time without fear of losing her. She is willing to submit to this because of the tremendous advantage of having a man, not only financially, but also from the point of view of social prestige. Women, in describing the ideal husband, mention first of all the ability to earn a good living, but also kindness, generosity, and affection. Men, on the other hand, desire obedience, fidelity, a pleasing physical appearance, ability to cook well, and industriousness. So long as a husband continues to bring home an adequate income, he is in little danger of losing his woman, but if he should become lax in this, the other qualities become more important in holding her.

Many institutionalized patterns of behavior reflect this unequal position of men and women in regard to maintaining marital stability. Women who are attached to the same man are exceedingly jealous of each other, especially if they are young. If two of them happen to meet in the street, they hurl insults at each other while the friends and relatives of each prod her into actual combat. They may end up by being arrested for disturbing the peace. The man involved usually makes himself scarce at such times, but is not chastized for carrying on with both women. In fact, his reputation as a desirable partner may be enhanced. Aside from the actual participants in the fracas, no one is highly disturbed, and many derive a good chuckle from the situation. In the event of an arrest of one or both women, the matter is usually quickly settled "out of court" by the payment of a fine or bribe to the arresting official.

Women, on the other hand, are severely criticized by both sexes if they grant their favors to two or more men at the same time. Informants told me that this situation occurred occasionally, but always in secret. One of the men is the socially approved husband, the other the secret lover. Obviously, the lover is aware of the deception, while the husband is not.

When the situation is discovered, revenge is generally taken only upon the woman. She is nearly always abandoned by the wronged husband, usually after a severe beating and public denunciation. The woman may begin living openly with the lover after this, and, if such behavior is not too frequent, the society will eventually forget her disgrace. All male informants told me that they would think twice before aligning themselves with such a woman, for if she deceived one husband, it was very probable that she would deceive another. Yet during my field residence there were several instances in which such women did secure new partners.

The situation of inequality is also reflected by the tremendous number of magical devices believed to be effective in holding a man, or in gaining his affection. Comparable love magic for men is less common, although there are methods that a man may use to determine whether or not a woman is faithful to him.

The Carib man, then, plays an important, yet marginal, role in the Carib household. His importance, in a very real sense, depends upon the amount and stability of the financial contribution he is able to make. He finds himself in demand as a provider not only in his own natal group, but also among women with whom he has established a marital relationship. His attachment to his natal group, and the ties between him and his mother and sisters, is usually much stronger than that between him and his spouse, although real affection can and often does exist in the latter relationship. When he is out of a job, as is frequently the case, he finds himself far more welcome and secure among his maternal kin, who will feed and house him in spite of his inability to contribute for a time, whereas a wife is likely to leave him when he is financially embarrassed. His authority over women within the conjugal relationship, though stronger than that among those of his natal household, is nevertheless more impermanent and less constant. Although he may have little to say or do in the socialization of his own children, he can be a real force in raising those of his sisters. This again is related to the instability of house-holds based upon conjugal ties, for when they break up the children almost invariably remain with the mother. Thus, the group of children in a man's mother's or sister's household remains the same, while his own children, probably belonging to several different women, will be scattered.

I have already noted certain patterns of behavior which exist between siblings of the opposite sex. In addition, it should be noted that the fact of having a common mother is the most important bond, regardless of whether or not the father is the same. Children of the same father also consider themselves to be siblings, and are generally good friends if they live within the same village, but the ties are not so strong, and they seldom reside together, either as children or as adults. During the course of the field work a man visited the household within which I was living, and I was informed that he was related to the young adults in the household through having a common father. He was accepted, fed, and housed, and the children within the group looked to him with respect, as did the elderly female head of the house who was the mother of the others. She did not seem to resent his presence, although the general atmosphere among all concerned seemed to be more friendly than affectionate. Such individuals are referred to as "outside children" by their paternal half-siblings. Although this term is used commonly throughout the West Indies to refer to illegitimate children, among the Carib it was frequently used in situations where legitimacy was not a meaningful issue. Thus, women and their children might use it to refer to any children of the father (or fathers) by *other women*. This usage seems to me to be another reflection of the solidarity of the unit composed of a woman and her children.

A man's wife or wives may or may not be on friendly terms with his maternal relatives. This depends on individual circumstances, such as the former relations between the man's relatives and those of the girl, the circumstances of the marriage itself, whether the girl has a good moral reputation within the community, and the manner in which she behaves herself after the union. In any case, the arrival of children often creates a friendlier atmosphere between a new bride and her husband's maternal kin. Most mothers are eager to cement relations with this group for the sake of their children. Godparents are quite often chosen among the father's maternal kin, thus reinforcing the kinship bonds already existing. If her husband's mother and sisters live within the same village, the mother makes a point of taking her child to visit on Sundays and holidays, and she often leaves the child with his father's kin for a day or so when she has business elsewhere. In all but the most exceptional cases, a child will always be welcome in the home of his father's maternal relatives, even after his parents are no longer formally attached to each other.

As a child grows older he may gradually drift away from his father's kinfolk. As this happens, his rights and obligations within the group tend to be obscured and forgotten. Only if he maintains friendly relations with them until adulthood — attending the appropriate ancestor rites, visiting often, helping with some domestic tasks, and occasionally bringing gifts — can he expect a share in his father's property or a warm welcome in the households of his father's kin.

Five

~~~~~~

DOMESTIC STRUCTURES
OF BLACK CARIB SOCIETY

~~~~~~

THE HOUSEHOLD

THE household among the Carib is composed of men, women, and children bound together by kinship ties of various kinds. Its membership fluctuates continually, not only with the birth of children, death of various members, and the loss of young people through marriage, but also through the extremely common practices of "loaning" children, divorce, double residence of members (especially men), absentee labor, and "visiting." A census taken in November, 1956, revealed seven household forms in Livingston. These forms and their frequencies are shown in Table 3.

Inquiries into the life histories of various individuals support the view that any given person will participate in several of these forms in the course of his life, and that any given household (defined by location) will go through several trans-

TABLE 3

FREQUENCY OF VARIOUS HOUSEHOLD FORMS
IN LIVINGSTON, GUATEMALA, 1956

	Type of Household	Number of Households	Percentage of Total
	1. One woman plus children	84	23.20%
	2. Two or more women plus children	40	11.05
Consanguineal households	3. One or more women, plus children, plus consanguineally related male(s)	40	11.05
	Subtotal	164	45.30
	4. One couple plus children, at least one of which is the child of both	104	28.73%
	5. One couple — no children	49	13.54
Affinal households	6. One couple plus children of the woman only	27	7.46
	7. One couple plus children belonging to neither	18	4.97
	Subtotal	198	54.70
	Total	362	100.00%

formations of form over time. Because of this fact, it is difficult to isolate any one household form as being typical of the society as a whole. I shall try to show which forms are most common and indicate under what circumstances each arises.

The household is the basic domestic and social unit of the society. It provides for the protection and socialization of the children, but in many cases it is not adequate to provide for the procreation of children. This results from the fact that often where men are present they either are beyond the age of reproduction or are related to the women by kinship ties which prohibit sexual union.

The most enduring relationships are, first, that between mother and child and, second, that between siblings. Marriages are entered into lightly, with little or no ceremony, and are brittle and unenduring. Thus, the core of the household group, regardless of fluctuations which take place, is a woman and her children, or two or more related women plus children of all of them. These consanguineous groups may consist of a mother and her daughter plus children of both, or a group of sisters and their children. The adult male members of the household will at various times include sexual and economic partners of the women, but they generally take up temporary residence or merely visit, spending anywhere from one night to a few months in the household. These men may then go off to another town to work, reside for a short period with another woman, or go back to their "home," by which they usually mean the house of their mother or sisters.

Most frequently then, the adult male members of the household group who reside there with any permanence will be sons or brothers of the central core of women. These men may or may not have female partners and children living in other houses in the same or another village.

Ideally, permanent monogamy, neolocal residence, and the nuclear family are held to be the most desirable forms. However, these ideals are seldom achieved in this society. As shown in Table 3, about 30 per cent of the household groups in Livingston *superficially* conform to these patterns, but the inconstant nature of even these groups may be seen by the fact that in the majority of cases (in categories 4, 6, and 7) the children in such household groups include those of the woman with a man or men now absent. Therefore, even though the household group in this instance happens to form a nuclear family, it is seldom a permanent group, apt to shatter at any moment for various reasons to be discussed below.

Form 5, one couple with no children, is also a fairly temporary grouping, sometimes consisting of a very young couple who as yet have no children or, more often, of very old people whose children have all gone away or died. In most of these cases the household will be part of a larger compound including kinfolk with whom the couple have daily contacts. Household groups often tend to split or segment when they become too large to live in one house. In this case an extra house will be built, and if there happens to be a couple without children, or a single person without children, they will most probably be housed there.

Such compounds are not consumption units, although, as sometimes occurs, an old person may sleep alone in a separate structure but eat at the house of a nearby daughter or sibling. In most cases, however, the compounds are loose associations of households, the members of which are usually related in the maternal line. In a sense they form small mutual aid societies, each household helping the others in repairing houses, working in the fields, taking care of the children, running errands, and doing domestic chores, and also helping out in times of sickness and death. The compound yard is the site of after-supper sessions of gossiping for the women and games for the children, the men generally convening on the beach or in the local taverns.

Each household operates independently in terms of its domestic budget, although gifts of food are exchanged from time to time with other households in the compound. If one of the men goes fishing, he is obligated to distribute fish to his maternal relatives, many of whom will be living in the same compound, and thus the obligation stemming from a sense of kinship is reinforced by common location. Figure 3 shows the layout of one such compound and the relationships among the people living there.

Institutions and customs which contribute toward the fluctuation of the household group include the practice of temporary or permanent loaning of children, discussed in Chapter IV. When a marriage is terminated, children generally stay with the mother or with one of her maternal relatives. Exceptions to this practice may occur if the woman has several other children by another man. In this case, the father may choose to take his child or children and place them with one of his sisters or with his mother rather than contribute money toward their support which might be used by the mother for her other children as well. In most of these cases, however, a father will continue to provide something toward the support of his chil-

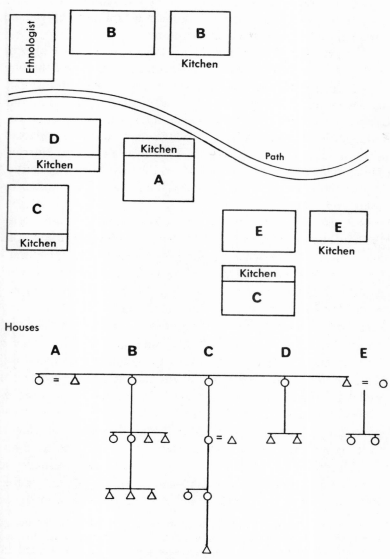

Sketch map of Carib compound

dren while they remain with their mother. This practice in Livingston has recently been reinforced by Guatemalan law. Now a woman may go to court and demand a minimum allowance for each child acknowledged by the man.

The practice of double residence also has an effect in producing the varying types of household groups found among the Carib. By the term "double residence" I mean an instance in which an individual claims residence in more than one household group. Double residence for a man most often occurs within the same village, although many men are a part of a household unit in Livingston as well as in Puerto Barrios. This practice may take one of several forms. Most frequently, a man may divide his time between the house of his mother or sister and that of his "wife."

It is also very common for a man to divide his time between the households of two women unrelated to him. It is difficult at this point to decide what terminology to use for this phenomenon. I hesitate to term this polygyny, since the two "wives" usually do not accept each other, and since this form is not admitted as an ideal by the members of the society.[1] It would seem to be a *modified* form of monogamy in that the male will usually admit his double alliance, and his behavior toward both women involves sexual activity, economic cooperation, and, to an extent, common residence, although the wives are under separate roofs. The man also recognizes the children of both women equally. Informants told me that some women involved in such a relationship accept and like the arrangement, visiting back and forth, helping each other with household duties, sharing goods, and so forth. This acceptance seems to be more characteristic of the older women, although I am unable to explain why this should be so.[2] Among younger women the

[1] For this reason it was impossible to obtain statistics on the occurrence of double residence. Information on this custom was obtained through observation and through discussion with several trusted informants.

[2] In a personal communication, Keith Otterbein has suggested that

two involved are exceedingly jealous of each other, to the point of active and violent quarreling. The man stays clear of such a dispute, generally taking refuge in his mother's house or in a neighboring town until the affair blows over. Following M. G. Smith (1926b:202 *passim*), I will use the term "extra-residential" to refer to unions which do not involve common residence.

Marriage begun with a wedding recognized by Guatemalan law and the Catholic church is quite rare among the Caribs, although the overwhelming majority adhere to this religious faith. One informant explained this to me by saying that if a couple married and then found that they could not get along together, there was nothing to be done because the church forbids divorce. Also, if a man were living with two women and decided to marry one, the other would be jealous, for she would want to get married, too, and of course the church would not allow that either. Therefore, this informant felt that it is far better not to bother with marriage at all, or at least not until one has lived with a woman many years. However, partnerships which are entered into by men and women, though not termed "marriages" by the Carib when using English or Spanish, are socially recognized and approved relationships. Each partner in such a relationship refers to the other as "my partner," or "my man," or "my woman," in English or Spanish. In the Carib language one term, "*numari*" (spouse), is used, whether or not the relationship is sanctioned by law and the church. Another term, "*ninauna*," which according to Taylor (1951:76) means "my mistress," though rarely used today, apparently has lost this meaning and may be used interchangeably with *numari*.

Socially approved sexual alliances may take a variety of forms. The first such relationship entered into by a man and woman may involve some formality by following the tradi-

---

competition for the man's earnings may be more rife among younger women who have children to support. This seems reasonable, and is not inconsistent with my data.

tional pattern. In the past, when two young people decided they wanted to live together, the man went to a male relative older than himself and asked him to intercede for him with his father. This relative then went to the boy's father, and they discussed the matter. If they approved, the father consulted the boy's mother. The boy was expected to be fully capable of making a living in some way before they would grant their permission. In addition, the girl and her entire family had to meet the approval of the boy's family before permission was granted. Grounds for disapproval included extreme youth of the girl (less than sixteen to seventeen years of age), a reputation for lax sexual behavior on her part, "unluckiness" of her family (that is, frequent deaths, financial misfortunes, accidents, and the like), or a tradition of bad relations between the two families. If marriages previously contracted between the two families had not worked out, these were thoroughly discussed and evaluated. If it was thought that the breakups were due to the woman's misbehavior, the boy's family probably would not have approved the proposed new alliance.

Finally, if the boy's family approved, his father spoke with the father of the girl. Her family then went through the same procedure until a decision was reached. If her family approved, a meeting was arranged between the couple and their respective families. Then the adults questioned the young couple as to their love for each other and their intentions to live together peacefully. They also warned them of the great step they were taking and of the responsibilities each would have toward the other and toward their future children. If the couple still expressed a desire to be married, definite arrangements proceeded. The boy decided on the date for the consummation and informed the girl's father. The date was often set as far in advance as five years. Long periods are now less common, although several older informants told me that they were usual in the past, when a man might travel as far as Honduras to ask for a girl, then return to clear fields, make dugout canoes or other articles for sale, work at wage labor, or in some other way earn enough to build a house, buy furniture, and set up housekeeping. In the meanwhile he and the girl would be betrothed, and he would be responsible for furnishing her with clothes and personal adornments.

In the past, when the time for the fulfillment of the contract arrived, the young man returned to present the girl's mother with a set of mahogany bowls of various sizes and a set of mortars and pestles. During the engagement period he had made these, as well as another set for the later use of his bride and himself. Sometimes it was required that he build a house and clear a field for his mother-in-law. When these things were accomplished, he could have the girl. There was no special ceremony — at least not in the memory of any of the informants living today. One informant told me of the former custom of making a virginity test. The first sexual contact between the young couple took place in the girl's house. All the relatives of the two sat in an adjoining room and waited until the boy returned with a white cloth which had been placed on the bed or mat. If it was spotted with blood, everyone showed signs of approval and congratulated the boy and both sets of parents. If it was not, the girl and her family suffered disgrace.

After this the girl stayed in bed for one week with a cloth over her head and her ears stuffed with cotton. She could not work, and her diet was limited. The new husband slept in the girl's house and attended to his new wife, but he could not have sexual contact with her again during this week. At the end of the week the couple moved into their own house or, more often, set up housekeeping with one or the other set of parents.

At the present time this procedure for accomplishing a marriage has changed considerably. Parts of the old procedure remain as an ideal pattern, which is actually followed only by a few. The boy is theoretically supposed to ask permission, and this is often accomplished by writing a letter to the girl's father, a document which will be kept and treasured in her family thereafter. Some syncretism with customs of Spanish or

English origin seems involved here. The couple must still experience the testimonial meeting with their respective relatives. The waiting period is usually cut considerably, now lasting from two weeks to a year at the most. The handmade mahogany bowls and mortars have been replaced by inexpensively purchased dishes. Clearing a field and building a house for the girl's mother, the virginity test, and the week-long seclusion for the bride have disappeared altogether.

Today most couples dispense with all the above procedure and simply elope. It is common for a girl just to disappear from home; after a week or so her family discovers that she is now living with a man in the same village or a nearby one. In most cases the family disapproves of this procedure but seldom interferes unless the girl is very young, that is, under sixteen. Generally it is not considered proper for a man to be married before twenty, nor a girl before sixteen. Usually the couple is older than this. My census shows that most young couples are about the same age, the man being perhaps a year or two older. Among slightly older couples the man is often the girl's senior by ten years or more.

The society's attitude toward alliances without the sanction of the law or church is acceptance *if* the father recognizes the children which result. Even if the two never actually reside in the same house, the union is considered proper so long as the man contributes to the support of the woman and children. When the union is terminated, if the father simply deserts the woman and her child or children, there is some public disapproval of both parties. This takes the form of gossip, and perhaps mild ostracism. If a woman makes several short-term alliances which result in children unrecognized by the various fathers, she acquires a reputation of being rather stupid, hard to live with, and somewhat loose morally. She may eventually have difficulty finding a man with whom she can establish even a semi-permanent relationship. A man's reputation may also be hurt if he repeatedly begets children without recognizing them. Even though it becomes more difficult for him to establish real marital alliances, he rarely has difficulty in finding women with whom he can enter into a sexual union. In connection with this, it should be noted that the ratio of men to women during the childbearing years is at the present time about one to six in Livingston (see Table 2, 55). This appears to be largely due to the absence of men performing wage labor.

Marriage sanctioned by the church and state tends to be limited to members of the small, financially better-off class, or to older people who have been living happily together for many years.[3] Such older couples may decide to legalize their marriage in order to provide security in inheritance for their children or, more importantly, to raise their social position in the community. Formal marriage of this type is a lengthy and expensive procedure, for it requires two ceremonies — one at the civil offices and one at the church — ordinarily followed by a feast and dance given in the home of the woman. The whole ceremony may take three days.

No mode of divorce for legal marriage is recognized. But dissolution of other marital unions is easy and frequent, and involves no formal ceremony. When a woman takes the action, if she has resided in a separate house with her husband, she usually waits until the man has gone away for a few days, then she cleans the house, washes his clothes, and leaves, taking her children and her belongings to the house of her mother or her sister. When the man returns and finds the house empty, he realizes that their association has been ended. If they are living in the woman's house, she has more difficulty in making the break. She cannot simply throw her husband and his belongings out of the house. Usually he leaves when she dismisses him, but if he resists, all she can do is make life miserable enough for him to leave of his own accord.

[3] Class divisions, not treated extensively in this study, are based on wealth, amount of education, and moral character of the individuals. Class status does not necessarily descend in family lines; it must be acquired or maintained by each individual in his adulthood.

If a man wishes to divorce his wife, he may order the woman to leave the house, if it belongs to him. Informants say, however, that eviction of a woman who has children is rare, unless the woman has been caught in adultery, which is the strongest, though not the most frequent, motive for divorce. Usually the man simply moves out of the house himself, leaving it for the use of the woman and her children. If the couple are living in a house belonging to the woman, the man may simply take his belongings — usually when the woman is absent — and leave.

In any case, a man continues to be responsible for his children financially throughout their childhood. Even if the woman marries again, the second husband will not usually wish to support another man's children. He will perhaps tolerate their living with their mother in his house, but he will expect the mother to provide for their support, either through the father of the children or by her own or the children's efforts.

There definitely exists a double standard in respect to divorce, remarriage, and sex. There is a feeling that a woman should not, with honor, have sexual relations with more than one man during her lifetime, unless the first husband dies. This ideal is rarely adhered to. Second alliances are usually tolerated for the woman, for there is also an attitude, somewhat counterbalancing the other, that a woman needs to have a man to take care of her financially. In 1930 a club was organized which attempted to provide ways for women left husbandless to support themselves and their children cooperatively in order to avoid the "dishonor" of living with another man. This club did not keep women from remarrying when the opportunity presented itself, but it undoubtedly helped those women who were unable to find another man to support them. As mentioned earlier, a woman invites gossip and disapproval only after she loses several marital partners. If she has been instrumental in getting rid of her man — by being extremely argumentative or by actually hitting him — she will find it even more difficult to find another.

Attitudes toward men's behavior, however, are quite different. As long as a man continues to recognize and support his children, he does not gain the disapproval of the society, regardless of how many unions he has had. According to informants' accounts, most men seem to have had at least two, and quite often as many as six, partners.

In regard to sanctions, I have termed any union a marriage if the ethnic group consider the children of such a union to be legitimate children of the couple in question. This criterion raises the question of the meaning of the term "legitimate." Among the Carib, who own little, if any, productive land and who have no concept of private or corporate ownership of fishing rights, inheritance rights refer only to house sites, money, and personal belongings. Therefore, "legitimacy" does not only or primarily concern the child's right to inherit property from his father or father's kin. In addition, it involves the right to receive hospitality from the father's group, a right to identify a man as his father, the right to seek financial or other assistance from him, and the rights and obligations involved in the ancestor ceremonies. All of these rights may be seen to derive directly from the "ethnic" ideals and customs and have little to do with the larger society of the outside world.

Among the Carib, the establishment of legitimacy depends upon the man's verbal recognition of paternity. At present, however, with increasing frequency a father is expected to register the child as his own with the municipal authorities. This procedure is preferred by most women, for it gives them a right enforced by the external, non-Carib society to demand financial assistance from the father in raising the child even if the couple later separate. In addition, it secures to the child the legal right to inherit property from the father in the possible event that the latter's kin might dispute this right in the future. Thus, it may be seen that when property rights are involved, the Caribs, whose indigenous system cannot always handle possible altercations, turn to the laws and courts of the country in which they reside.

One may divide all marital unions into types, depending upon sanction. One type includes those sanctioned by a Christian church and by the national government. In both Guatemala and Honduras the only ceremony legally recognized is that performed by the civil authorities. Therefore, Christian marriage involves two ceremonies — one in the municipal office, followed by another in the church. Since all Caribs are nominally Catholics, and since this church does not recognize any marriage performed by another agency, both ceremonies are always performed. This type of marriage I have termed "Western," in order to emphasize that it is an element of social organization stemming directly from the larger society within which the Carib live. An important factor is that unions so sanctioned have the recognition of persons outside the Carib ethnic group itself.

The second type of sanction is that granted by the smaller, strictly Carib, society. I have already noted and described procedures by which a couple may achieve recognition of a marriage in this way. Some of these unions are extremely short-lived, but others may last a lifetime. I see little usefulness in classifying them on this basis, however, since at the outset these unions are functionally the same, the differences among them being definable primarily in terms of the type of residence involved. This type of sanction I have termed "ethnic," since it provides legality only within the group itself. One instance will illuminate the difference between the two sanctions. An informant was considering legal, Christian (what I have termed "Western") marriage at the age of forty after having mated with five different women, at times with two or three simultaneously. He was planning a trip to the United States, and, he pointed out, "You can hardly go traveling about the world with a woman who is not your wife." Later his plans for traveling changed, and I heard no more of marriage plans.

Because of the nature of the customs and attitudes surrounding these various types of marital bonds and residence patterns, it was impossible to gather accurate statistics which would give the frequency of each type. In taking the census I was able to obtain quantitative information only on unions in which the couple resided together. On the other hand, it is highly probable that in many cases the same man was reported as residing in two or more households as a husband-father, or as a husband-father in one and a brother-son in another. In a society as large as this, it is impossible for one investigator in a year's time to gain the confidence of every individual. For this reason I do not feel that the census figures are accurate regarding the number of marriages. Nevertheless, a total of only sixty-five legal marriages was reported, and this figure is, if anything, exaggerated because of the high amount of prestige associated with this type of marriage. Most of these marriages were associated with neolocal residence, and in the majority the couple was over forty years of age.

Those Caribs who enter into Western-type marriage usually fall into what may be termed the local upper class. Generally the men have jobs which give them a substantial income and allow them to settle down in one place permanently. Jobs of this type include white-collar or skilled-labor jobs, such as mechanic, typesetter, clerk, janitor, and the like. Many couples in this category actually leave their home village and go to live in Guatemala City, Tegucigalpa, and other non-Carib towns and cities. (Naturally, such couples were not included in the census of Livingston.) Occasionally, informants told me that they had married because their employers encouraged them to do so, even though they had been living with their wives for some time beforehand and had several children. There is definitely an element of prestige involved in marrying according to Western standards, regardless of whether the couple continues to reside together. It costs a great deal more money to hold a Western wedding, which involves expense for suitable clothing, court and church fees, food, liquor, and music for the large party which follows the ceremonies.

Extraresidential Western marriages are encountered fairly often. Again, it was not possible to gather statistics on these. Many such cases involve persons who had at one time left Carib society and then later returned. Quite often they occur when a man has a permanent job in one of the outside towns, but for some reason does not take his wife along with him. She may be needed to help at home, the husband may not be able to afford to have her with him in the town where he is working, or the couple may no longer wish to live together. He may visit her occasionally; he continues to contribute to her support, but he does not consider her home to be his. Since the Catholic church does not sanction divorce of persons it marries, it may happen that each member of the union is actually residing with another sexual partner. Usually outside unions of this type are not approved by the society at large — the married woman especially is criticized for changing partners. There is some feeling that if two people actually marry according to Western law, they should remain together regardless of what happens. A woman married in such a way and then deserted retains the prestige conferred by the marriage only if she remains aloof from other men thereafter.

Extraresidential mating would appear to be the most frequent of all marital arrangements. This seems to bear some relation to the age of the man and woman concerned; that is, young people just starting out, though they may live together in one or the other's natal unit for a time, quite frequently continue living separately, with the man visiting his wife at night. Later, when they can afford it, they will build a house of their own. On the other hand, as they grow older, if they have not changed partners before this, the woman may return to her mother's home while the man continues to live in the house. Or a woman may continue to live in the house her husband built for her while he moves to another house. Or he may, as noted previously, take up double residence with two women, alternating his time between them. Another factor which leads to duolocality is the man's working full time in one of the port towns and maintaining a house or room there, while the woman continues to live in the village, either with her maternal relatives or in a house provided by her husband.

It cannot be emphasized too strongly that the life history of any given individual will exhibit a number of the different situations described here. Very seldom, if ever, do a man and woman marry, settle down in one type of residence, and remain there for the rest of their lives. The various kinds of household groups discussed above arise through the establishment of the different kinds of marital arrangements and events which follow them, including births, adoptions, divorces, and migration.

It is argued here that the concrete structures called households, in all their varieties, may be best understood in terms of the interrelationships arising between adult men and women, which in themselves seem to be dependent primarily upon the economic situation. Ideally, a man becomes more secure financially as he grows older, and, if this happens, he is more likely to set up a neolocal household with his wife and marry her according to Western tradition. This is especially apt to happen if his job is of the sort which allows him to leave the local scene and enter into the society of the world at large. However, it cannot be said that the various types of marriage and residence form a fixed sequential pattern through which all, or even most, individuals progress. Children do not necessarily follow the same pattern as either parent — in the absence of the accumulation of great amounts of inheritable property, the children must achieve social position on the basis of their own abilities and luck. Throughout life, the household type in which Black Caribs happen to be living at any particular time will generally be directly related to the amount and source of cash income they can command — through labor if they are males, and through males if they are females.

NUCLEAR FAMILY, HOUSEHOLD,
AND EXTENDED UNILATERAL FAMILY

As yet I have deliberately avoided the use of the term "family" in speaking of Carib social units, for in view of the usual definition of this term in anthropology, it might be questioned as to whether such concrete units exist as typical structures in this society. Of the units I have termed affinal households," there is little doubt that the term "family" fits as well as "household." But how are we to treat those units within which no husband-father figure resides?

Elsewhere I have suggested that the family be defined as a group of people bound together by kinship ties, between at least two of whom there exists a conjugal relationship recognized by the society in which they live (Solien 1960). This conjugal pair, plus their offspring, forms the nuclear family. Other types of family may be defined as extensions of the nuclear family, each type being identified by the nature of the relationship between the conjugal pair and the other members.

The household, on the other hand, implies common residence, economic cooperation, and socialization of children. Although the members of the household may be bound by kinship relationships, no particular type of tie is necessarily characteristic. In any given society a particular family may or may not form a household. The Carib data show that in some societies it is necessary to make a rigid distinction between the two concepts, "family" and "household."

The nuclear family unit among the Carib may be scattered in several different households. For example, the husband-father may be living with his own mother; one or more children may be with their maternal relatives or with non-Caribs, while the mother may be working and "living in" as a maid in one of the port towns. Some observers may then assert that under such circumstances this no longer constitutes a family unit. However, if the nature of the personal interrelationships among the group members is considered, it may be seen that there exists a pattern of affective and economic solidarity among them. It is true that many such groups are extremely brittle and unstable, but they do exist for varying lengths of time.

In addition to the nuclear family, which may be united or dispersed, one may isolate three other types of kinship categories among the Carib, some of which may be called groups. The first of these is what I shall call the "extended unilateral family." The following relatives are normally included from the point of view of any given individual: mother, father, siblings of the mother, mother's mother, mother's father, own siblings, mother's sisters' children, own children, children of own sisters, own grandchildren. Note that this set of relatives has been differentiated from that termed the household. This extended unilateral grouping may or may not be (usually is not) identical with that found within the household. However, in any one household, one may find *some* of these relatives, but rarely persons outside of the list. The extended family may be considered as the larger category from which the household is constituted. As such, it is *not* a group in and of itself, but merely a set of relatives who are *potential* residential associates. I should stress that this is an analytic category, isolated on the basis of observed behavior among the Caribs as indicated by the census materials and case histories. I found no word in the Carib language to refer to any such "grouping." I have called this the extended *unilateral* family because, aside from Ego's own father (or mother's later husband), the category is composed only of *maternal* kin. Among the Carib the distinction between "mother's relatives" (*tiduheyu nuguchu*) "father's relatives" (*liduheyu nuguchi*) is an important one, and although the latter category may furnish potential important linkages, the household tends to be made up of some aggregation of the former.

THE PERSONAL KINDRED

Another category of relatives, which I shall call the personal kindred, theoretically consists of all the descendants of an individual's great-grandparents, although in most cases a person will not recognize all of these, nor will he know the exact linkage which binds him to many of those whom he does recognize. Clearly, this category includes all of those relatives in the extended unilateral family plus many more, drawn from both the mother's and the father's sides. This category, as it is generally understood, forms no distinct body or corporate group, but is relative to each sibling group (Davenport 1959; Freeman 1961; Goodenough 1962). Leopold Pospisil and William Laughlin have argued that the kindred must be considered as more than "merely a social category since its members may — and on specified occasions do — come together and act in unison on behalf of Ego, their common link" (1936:187). However, among the Black Carib I found *no* occasion upon which such groups came together on the behalf of Ego *except after his death*. Funerals and ninth-night wakes were attended by persons drawn from this category of relatives, many of whom might never have met before. Since these persons were not bound together by any mutual rights and obligations, I find it difficult to think of them as constituting even a "quasi group." Neither is there any consistency as to the ways in which individual Caribs behave relative to persons in this category. The number of degrees of relationship recognized vary considerably from person to person. Relatives living within the same settlement tend to recognize each other over wider spans of relationship than those living in widely separate communities. However, the frequent traveling from one community to another, both in the past and at the present time, tends to keep even these ties from dying altogether. The major function of this category of relatives seems to lie in the area of hospitality — an individual can always count on temporary food and shelter from any member of his personal kindred.

Informants agree that when visiting a previously unknown town, they might not be aware of the names of potential relatives there. But, armed with the names of one's great-grandparents and grandparents, plus their birthplaces, it is usually possible to find kinfolk. Once a legitimate linkage has been established, etiquette demands furnishing hospitality to such persons. On my survey of Carib villages in British Honduras and Honduras, I was furnished with a list of names of ancestors of my host family in Livingston, and I never failed to find kinfolk of these people in any village.

It is not surprising, in a society in which marital ties are so ephemeral and unstable, that affines are not included in this same category. One's current or past spouse's relatives *may* actually offer hospitality, but this is not seen as a kinship obligation, only a courtesy.

THE NONUNILINEAR DESCENT GROUP

In addition to the kinship categories described above, there exists another, of a type which has recently attracted a great deal of attention from anthropologists (see Befu 1963; Blehr 1963; Davenport 1959; Goodenough 1955 and 1962; Murdock 1960; Sahlins 1958; and Scheffler 1966, among others). Some have preferred to call this type of structure a cognatic descent group, an ambilineal descent group, or a ramage (see Scheffler 1966 for a review of the different terminological usages). I will use the term "nonunilinear descent group," following Goodenough (1955) and Davenport (1959), since it seems clear enough, and is close to the phrase originally used in this manuscript.

All of the members of this group are descended from a known common ancestor through *any* line, whether through males or females. The line of descent may cross over from male to female or vice versa in any generation. However, all of the possible descendants of a given individual will not be included, for the membership of the group is restricted by some additional factor outside the kinship system itself. Conversely, an individual at birth has the potential right of belonging to as many groups as he has ancestors, and since he derives this initial right of belonging by virtue of the concept of *descent*, it seems appropriate to use the term "descent group" here. Such groups, although capable of forming discrete, corporate units, do not necessarily have mutually exclusive memberships. Among the Carib, for example, an individual — especially early in life — might validate his membership in two or three or more such groups. Obligations among members of these groups are second only to those within the household and compound. Actually, the latter may be thought of as *minimal* cognatic descent groups, crystallizing around what Pehrson called a "sibling alliance unit" (1954:20). The descent group is usually larger than this, however, and includes nonresidents. Exchanges of gifts (usually food), help in housebuilding, harvesting, and the processing of manioc, and so forth, take place regularly among members of this group, regardless of place of residence, unless members live in different towns. When the latter is the case, members have an obligation to attend funerals and wakes on the ninth night after death, to give assistance when other members are dangerously ill, to send money in times of financial crisis, and, most importantly, to participate in and help pay for the rites given in honor of the particular ancestor from whom the group takes its orientation.

A description of one such group and its behavior will be illustrative of such descent groups among the Carib. In the compound in which I lived were five houses. In these lived a group of brothers and sisters, their children, grandchildren, and one great-grandchild. The husbands of the three sisters in the original group were not residents of the area. The eldest brother's wife divided her time between this compound and her own, where lived her mother and siblings. She was not an integrated member of this compound. The other brother had a wife from Honduras, who had no close relatives in Livingston. She had become an integrated member of this group, a status which was reinforced by the institution of *compadrazgo*. She was godmother to one of the children in the compound, and her own children's godmothers were also settled within the compound. No other affinally related individuals had become permanently functioning members of the group. Although the adult female children of the three sisters lived in the compound, together with their children and occasionally with their husbands, the adult male children either had left the area entirely or had wives living elsewhere while they themselves remained with the group. As for the children of the two brothers, the younger had only small children, while those of the elder brother had all left the compound when they grew up.

The five brothers and sisters had inherited the compound from their mother, who had received it from her father. Beyond this no one remembers. The group described above differs from a unilinear descent group in that when any really important matters are to be considered, the children of the brothers, as well as of the sisters, are consulted. This group acted together in deciding matters such as how much rent should be charged me (although the woman who owned my house received this rent in full). Catches of fish were distributed among them, and they helped each other in times of sickness and death.

Although this group functioned as a mutual aid group in many day-by-day matters, it also was bound together by the fact that all of its members might eventually lay claim to the house and garden sites on which the compound stood. This circumstance, common in other West Indian societies as well, is the additional factor which restricts the membership of the nonunilinear descent group.

Although the nonunilinear descent group is still a functioning structure in Black Carib society, there is some evidence to indicate that it is unable to handle some situations regarding disputed inheritance rights. Obviously, all individuals will have many possible groups in which they may claim membership. I have shown in a previous publication (Solien 1959b) that the cult of the ancestors operates to sanction and reinforce the solidarity of the nonunilinear descent group. Individuals who do not cooperate in the rites held for a given ancestor may have difficulty establishing their rights to membership in the group counting descent from this particular ancestor. In addition to lending support to such rites, in the form of active participation and financial aid, individuals in the group are expected to help other members in sickness and death, and to render assistance to each other in various domestic and economic tasks.

At the present time many individuals seem to fail to behave in the proper fashion, yet they wish to lay claim to what they feel are their rights of inheritance in regard to land or money. Many such individuals, their claims being rejected by other heirs, now take their cases to court. If they are able to prove to the satisfaction of the judge, who is the representative of the national legal structure, that they are indeed lawful heirs, they will be awarded a share in the disputed property. These decisions are respected by those Caribs concerned (though not without a good deal of complaining and bad feeling), for the authority and strength of the Western legal system have long been recognized by members of the Carib ethnic group as a whole. Such instances, of course, serve to weaken the structure of the nonunilinear descent groups, and may point to a coming trend toward increasing individualization and dependence upon legal sanctions lying outside the strictly Carib frame of reference. As such, this trend may be seen as an indication of the degree of acculturation to Western civilization.

Six

~~~~~~

CROSS-CULTURAL COMPARISONS

~~~~~~

H AVING examined the structure and operation of the consanguineal household among the Black Carib, I now turn to the problem of explanation. Anthropology has long depended upon the comparative approach as a means of testing hypotheses developed from observations of a single society or culture. The classic procedure has been to take the particular feature in which one is interested and to seek to examine its occurrence in other societies as reported in the literature, comparing and contrasting its form, function, and development elsewhere with the situation perceived in one's own data. The features so compared have included acts, objects, ideas, complexes of such things and events, and constructs based upon our observations of such things and events and the apparent interrelationships among them. These constructs have included "patterns," "analytic structures," "organizations," "systems," and many other such concepts. Naturally, not all investigators have conceived their problems or defined their methodologies in exactly the same way, and variations are clearly discernible among those with different points of view throughout the history of anthropology. However, at some point, most anthropologists have attempted to draw comparisons between and among different sociocultural systems. This accomplishes several things. First of all, it enables one to know whether (or to what degree) one's own data appear to be unique in the world. Second, it permits a sorting out of the variables so that one may better construct a working hypothesis which attempts to express the relationships between variables. One of the underlying assumptions of this methodology is that similar forms have common historical origins, or have developed as responses to similar circumstances in the social and natural environment, or both.

One of the now obvious difficulties which has long plagued the social scientist is the suspicion that he may be comparing unlike things, and thus may reach spurious, meaningless, or untrue conclusions in regard to whatever it is he wishes to "explain." In part this problem seems to derive from different ways of perceiving the data, or from differences in the ways we abstract from the data in arriving at our analytical constructs, or a combination of these. Lacking a rigorous and well-defined methodology, it is important that we view both our own and others' "morphological types" with caution. Furthermore, even if we have sufficient evidence to feel that we are in fact dealing with similar forms, we must not necessarily assume that they have everywhere developed in precisely the same way. However, in our search for explanations, an understanding of the ways in which superficially different processes are in fact similar as formative or adaptive mechanisms would seem to be an important goal.

Therefore, in the discussion which follows, I have attempted to test my hypothesis concerning the development of the consanguineal household against what data concerning this form I could find.

AFRICA

Literature on the effects of urbanization and industrialization in Africa is vast; studies range over a period of twenty-five years. Tremendously varied circumstances make generalizations hazardous. In addition to different local situations due to different company policies, and others which originate in variations in native culture, reports vary also according to the points of view of the investigators who have reported on urbanization and industrialization in Africa. Different investigators examine distinct kinds of questions. Data on family systems, which are rarely a central concern, are seldom comparable. We find ourselves wishing we knew just who lives with whom, and the relationships involved. Nevertheless, there are a few things which stand out and which are of importance to my study. In some cases I have had to resort to reconstruction on the basis of mere "clues," a procedure which is admittedly dangerous. Inference of the existence of certain elements in a society where certain other elements are recorded, however, seems justified, if cautiously pursued, on the grounds that both groups of elements go together in a functional system. By making such inferences, I increase the number of societies that can be compared. In the discussion which follows, it is hoped that the reader will bear these preliminary remarks in mind.

The most important mechanism by which Africans have gradually become incorporated into the orbit of Western civilization is migrant wage labor. This is true in all parts of Negro Africa, although there are areas (for example, in East Africa) where money income is derived more from cash cropping than from wage labor. An important characteristic of the wage labor in Africa is that the worker must generally travel long distances from his home village to the labor centers, thus making it impossible to maintain frequent contact with his tribe or village. Another general characteristic is that wages are kept low, and housing, if provided, is almost always of the "bachelor quarters" type. These two factors, plus others stemming from the indigenous patterns of culture, have made it difficult, if not impossible, for men to take their families with them to the labor centers. In recent years in some areas, this pattern is changing, with companies providing family housing of various types. In the past, where migrancy occurred, it was almost universally the custom for the young men to go away to work for a few years, accumulate a certain amount of cash with which to pay taxes and brideprice, buy a few items, such as clothing for themselves and their families, perhaps a bicycle or a sewing machine, and then return to settle down into the traditional village life. I have called this "temporary, nonseasonal" migration.

This pattern still exists in many areas, but it has become increasingly more common for men to go away and become permanently separated from their home village. This process is often a gradual one, the men making fewer and fewer home visits through the years until their connections are finally terminated for all practical purposes. Until final separation occurs, the migration is of the kind I term "recurrent."

In studying the effects of recurrent migration upon family organization in Africa, it is first necessary to distinguish between the situation which arises in the home villages as they are depleted of males, and that in the labor centers themselves where families of any kind have not long been the pattern. The first obvious result of this migration is the unbalancing of the sex ratio, especially during the adult decades, a period which is of primary importance, not only for the economic system, but also for reproduction. The villages are left with a surplus of adult females, while males predominate in the urban centers. As we shall see, this undoubtedly has a great influence in determining the marriage patterns which emerge, and also, with other factors, the family patterns. Connected with this is another demographic characteristic of great importance: the urban areas include few old people of either sex. As the process of urbanization continues, there will probably be a trend toward a more normal distribution.

Most investigators agree that the rate of divorce in all urban centers is high. However, the figures often given in regard to marriage and divorce are difficult to evaluate because of the definition of marriage almost universally adhered to by the investigators themselves. Usually they recognize two primary types of marriage: civil or Christian (which I have classified as one), and marriage by Native Custom. The latter has long been recognized by Western administrators and is still usually more frequent than civil or church marriages. Nearly everywhere in Negro Africa, Native Custom involves the payment of brideprice in some form or another, plus certain ceremonial procedures carried out by the kin of the couple involved. In short, it tends to emphasize the linkage of two families or kin groups rather than the ties between two individuals. Marriage of any other sort is generally not termed "marriage" by the investigators, and as such is not included in statistics on numbers of marriages occurring. As we shall see, there is evidence that the Africans themselves are coming to recognize as legitimate another type of marriage, which is essentially a tie between individuals and not between kin groups. As such, it should be included by investigators when examining this aspect of social life. Such unions, it should be emphasized, are generally found only in urban areas, where broader kinship ties are weak or absent; if they occur in rural areas, the Africans do not usually regard them as being legitimate. The latter would then constitute a different category, and I would not regard them as marriages; but the former would come under my heading "ethnic marriage."

Concerning the increase of the rate of divorce in rural areas there seems to be some disagreement. Most writers claim that divorce is frequent, but many claim that it is no higher than before migrant labor existed (Phillips 1953:145, 155). Some suggest that marital infidelity is increasing in the villages, many women bearing children by lovers in the absence of their husbands, but that this has little effect on the total divorce rate (*ibid.*:106). Similarly, the amount of premarital conception

seems to be increasing in the rural areas and is no longer severely punished. Part of the explanation for this may be that
missionary and government influences have tended to destroy
the former sanctions against such behavior, and no new ones
have developed to take their place.

Polygyny, formerly fairly widespread in Africa, has declined, though it has not disappeared. Often a man will have
one wife in his home village, another wife in town. Polygyny
in the village itself still occurs, and, indeed, in some areas,
where plural wives give a man greater social prestige over his
fellows, it has increased with the general standards of living.
However, the most important factors operating to decrease the
amount of polygyny are missionary teaching and the change in
the economic system. Formerly, a wife was a definite asset,
and, as such, two were better than one, and so on. Now, however, especially in the urban areas, a wife is a definite liability.
She is completely dependent upon the man for her support and
often is unable to contribute in any way to the family income.
In some areas, it is true, she may find work as a domestic, or
she may engage in small trade, but these seem to be the exceptions rather than the rule. This condition, as will be seen
below, has definite bearing on the pattern of family types that
exist in the towns. On the other hand, the dearth of women in
towns makes it fairly easy for women to find husbands and
also gives the woman a certain security and independence, for
she knows that if she leaves her present husband or is deserted
by him, she will easily find another.

It has been pointed out that in the towns several categories
of mating exist. These range from prostitution through concubinage; from short-term unions with frequent changes in partner to life-long monogamous unions. The same woman may be
found successively in several of the different categories. Monica Hunter's evidence suggests that most of these types of unions are of a character that I would term true marriages
(UNESCO 1956:197). For example, she points out that
many women have a more or less permanent union with one

man, who may spend much of his time with the woman and largely support her while also having a legal wife in the country. Others have one lover after another, who may give presents or contribute to household expenses. Unfortunately, Hunter does not indicate the status of children of such unions, so that it is difficult to know how to classify them for our purposes. She notes that the number of such women is large in the urban community of East London, as shown by the fact that 56.7 per cent of non-European children born are illegitimate (*ibid.*: 198), but that does not help us here, for this figure includes any child not born from a marriage recognized by the government. It does not indicate their status from the African viewpoint. In cities other than East London, also, in addition to civil or church marriages and marriages by Native Custom, it seems that a type which I have called "ethnic" is becoming increasingly more frequent. These marriages are more common in the towns than in the villages where Native Law marriages still predominate. Whether the pattern of "ethnic" marriage in urban African centers can be shown to be similar to that described among the Carib, however, depends upon how various investigators define marriage. Before examining this problem more closely, I wish to deal with the possibility that family and household patterns like those of the Caribs exist in Africa.

Evidence on such family and household patterns is scanty in the literature. It appears that a group of consanguineally related adults plus children of the women all living together as a cooperative unit is a pattern that does not occur frequently. The case of Ashanti is interesting, for this matrilineal group has long had a residence pattern involving neolocality and duolocality (Fortes 1949:69–70, 75). There seems to be some question as to whether this pattern is aboriginal or has come about as a response to more modern economic conditions. In either case, it is relatively atypical for Africa, although the Uri of Ankole, who are largely dependent upon migrant wage labor, may be developing a similar pattern. Among the Uri, women turn for economic cooperation (in the villages) to other women — their mothers, sisters, and neighbors — and enter into sexual relationships with other men while their husbands are away (Phillips 1953:71). We are not told whether these women actually set up households together or whether they merely cooperate while living independently. In essence, this response to the situation is the same one that we see in Carib society today. As I have pointed out, relationships among adult Carib women often have an important economic function. Such cooperation among women appears to be one possible solution to a lack of men on the domestic scene.

Much is said in the literature on Africa concerning the economic role of women in the changing societies. Some writers claim that women have a greater economic independence than ever before, and have achieved the ability to free themselves from domination by their husbands. They have pointed out that the women's burden in maintaining the rural domestic economy — usually based on horticulture — is greater than ever before. Some women who cannot continue without having a man in the household to clear and to do the heavy work may turn to their own or their husband's relatives for assistance. Others hire this work done by unrelated persons and are thus able to maintain production without dependence upon kin.

In the urban areas too there is variation in the amount of economic independence women achieve. Some writers point out that women may more easily become economically independent in the towns, for they may secure work or engage in trade; while others claim that women are even more dependent upon males in the towns than they were in the villages, for in the absence of subsistence agriculture, the husband-wife unit is no longer a cooperative work unit. The situation obviously varies enormously and depends to a large extent upon the employment available to females in the different urban centers.

One point not generally recognized in the literature is the distinction between the economic independence of *women* as a class and the amount of independence any single woman can achieve on her own as a result of her earning ability. As shown among the Caribs, it is possible for women to carry on and support themselves and their children if enough of them band together for this purpose. However, a single woman with children finds it difficult, if not impossible, to function effectively as a mother, housekeeper, wage earner, and cultivator all in one. It appears that in Africa there are areas where women as a class (for example, in some urban areas where no work exists for females) cannot achieve much economic independence and must depend entirely upon males. On the other hand, there seem to be some urban situations in which women may find employment rather easily. This does not necessarily mean that each woman may then free herself completely from cooperation with all other adults, including husbands, brothers, parents, sisters, and so forth, even though she may now have greater freedom in moving from relationship to relationship. She may be able to live alone and support herself if she has no children, but as soon as these arrive she will find it necessary to form cooperative relationships with some other adult, whether or not she lives with that person. It is only in societies that provide institutions such as nursery schools, supervised playgrounds, and the like, that a woman with children can successfully carry on alone.[1]

In the rural areas of Africa, cooperative labor between males and females has been reduced. Females carry a larger burden than ever before, and thus as a class have greater economic independence. Again this varies from area to area, for apparently in some villages subsistence agriculture has been given up entirely, and the women depend exclusively on the contribution of money from the wage-earning men. Needless to say, this can only be effective in those areas where men still

[1] It is interesting to note that a social device of this sort existed in the West Indian slave plantations, whereby one or two women were excused from labor for the master to care for all the children, thus providing a type of "nursery school."

maintain close ties with their villages, sending back money frequently and returning themselves from time to time. Usually in these areas women do have some way of contributing to the cash income, often acting as middlemen in trade, making and selling beer, selling small amounts of garden produce, and so forth, but they remain dependent, for the most part, on the wages of the absent husbands (Phillips 1953:70; Schapera 1947:184; Westermann 1949:57). Whether or not they can achieve relative independence as a class, the same thing applies here as in town — a single woman with children cannot operate effectively alone.

It appears that in most rural cases the cooperative relationships follow old traditional patterns. In patrilineal societies one still finds that a women lives with her husband's kinfolk, cooperating with them long after her husband has migrated, whether temporarily or permanently (Barnes 1951:85; Schapera 1947:67, 185). In matrilineal societies which are also matrilocal, where women continue to live under the protection of their natal families, one would expect to find the closest similarity to the Carib situation. In such cases, however, the woman's father is likely to be present, and he would hold the greatest amount of familial authority.

In summary, although recurrent migrant wage labor in Africa has brought about changes in many aspects of social organization, the household types in the villages appear to have remained similar in structure to the aboriginal patterns. In towns, to which women have only recently begun to migrate, the nuclear family household is most typical, although this form is unstable and breaks up each time its basic conjugal tie is severed.

I conclude that household types in the range characteristic of the Black Caribs are not found typically in Africa. This is so in spite of the fact that migrant wage labor is widespread and plays a very important part in many economic systems in that continent. I believe that a number of factors can be shown to be effective in preventing the emergence of such a pattern.

The first is the force of aboriginal or traditional tribal structures. Until recently men who had spent several years in the labor centers tended to return home to settle down within the tribal pattern. According to Margaret Read (1942:610), "The great majority of 'temporarily urbanized' Africans maintain some links with their villages of origin, and this is the outstanding sociological phenomenon in the African labour situation today."

Although this situation has changed a great deal in the years since her statement was made, other workers in Africa have made similar observations. J. C. Mitchell points out that "it is quite possible for people to continue to follow tribal modes of behavior in some respects and participate in urban social relations in others" (1956:695).

It is clear from many studies that changes have occurred in such things as respect for the aged, the strength of wider kinship ties, and the stability of marriages. The experiences of men away from home do alter their behavior and attitudes toward the old patterns. However, as C. Sofer says, "It is clearly the indigenous social system which provides the fuller set of social institutions and instrumental and expressive cultural vehicles for the Africans" (Sofer 1956a:604). Even those Africans who stay away from home are not immune. Apparently a large proportion express the desire and expectation of returning home eventually, even though later circumstances may prevent them from actually doing so. Many Africans today go back to the village to secure wives according to traditional patterns. They pay brideprice, go through native ceremonies, and then move to the towns, taking their wives with them. Many African towns have neighborhoods and cooperative groups formed along the tribal lines, which provide an environment within which tribal customs and ideals may be more or less perpetuated. Most individuals in such circumstances govern their behavior and interpersonal relations according to those which receive tribal sanction. Bronislaw Malinowski expressed this point of view as follows: "Institutions endure because they satisfy an essential need of society. They can be suppressed, mutilated, deprived of some aspects, but they disappear only with destruction of the whole cultural identity of a people" (1945:53).

In discussing preconditions for the emergence of the consanguineal household pattern, I have postulated as necessary a society whose former cultural identity has been obscured, producing what I have termed a "neoteric" society. This occurred in the New World when large numbers of Africans from diverse cultural backgrounds were thrown together to form a new group with no single cultural identity. This also happened to the Black Caribs whose cultural origins are even more diverse than those of the former slaves. M. Fortes has used the term "discontinuity" to refer to this aspect of some social organizations. He says, "Discontinuity is exemplified in areas where military invasion and conquest and alien settlement on a big scale have occurred, or where a population of very diverse origins has been brought together forcibly in an alien land, as was the case with African slaves in the New World" (1949:55).

It is true that in some African urban centers one finds groups made up of individuals from diverse backgrounds. According to Sofer, in one residential area of Jinja, Uganda, the population consists almost entirely of immigrants who have come into the urban area as uprooted individuals. They experience a more extreme cultural shock than do persons who go where large numbers of their tribal brothers already reside. Sofer contrasts this area with another, Makende, in which the majority of the people are of the Soga tribe and in which many traditional patterns are maintained. In Makende there is a gradual breaking down of the extended family unit to accommodate to the new economic conditions which prevail, whereas in Bukesa, the social institutions must be built up from the single individual. Sofer feels that though the starting points are different, it is likely that after the present transitional period small-family units will be the most general under prevailing town conditions (Sofer 1956b:618).

The sex ratio characteristic of African urban areas probably significantly inhibits the emergence of consanguineal households. Among the Black Caribs and throughout the Caribbean generally, as well as among the United States Negroes, there is a general excess of females over males at all ages. If anything, this is more exaggerated in the towns than in rural areas (Roberts 1957:72). In Africa, on the contrary, men far outnumber women in the urban areas, the only areas in which one finds neoteric societies. This, combined with the premium placed upon women as mates in the towns, would probably militate against the appearance of many consanguineal households in the near future. In addition, at the present time women have few kinfolk in the towns to whom they may turn for assistance, and we have already emphasized the importance of this factor. The lack of traditional sanctions in these urban centers of uprooted individuals, plus the economic situation itself, will probably increase the amount of concubinage and changing of partners, but women will probably continue to look to nonrelated males for assistance, rather than to kin such as brothers, sisters, or parents. B. A. Pauw (1963) has recently described matrifocality among urban Bantu households in East London. It would be interesting to observe, if sex and age ratios in towns change in future years, whether a parallel change occurs in the type of adult cooperative relationships formed.

To summarize, consanguineal household systems are not generally found in Africa today, in spite of the prevalence of wage labor, urbanization, and detribalization.[2] The reasons for this lack are suggested to be as follows:

1. Traditional patterns of household composition are

[2] Mitchell suggests that "stabilization can be used for the settled residence of Africans in town, urbanization for the development of modes and standards of behavior peculiar to urban areas, and detribalization for the general change from tribal to Western standards of behavior" (1956:696).

usually maintained in the rural areas, in spite of the absence of men over long periods. Changes in marriage and divorce patterns do occur there, but it is most often reported that household composition remains the same, except for the absence of the husband. Since an extended family household of some type is almost universal in aboriginal Africa, the woman simply maintains traditional relationships with other members of his group.

2. In many urban areas the force of tradition and expectation of return to tribal life still remain important in determining family and household type. However, where changes do occur in these semi-traditional situations, coresiding nuclear families based on new forms of marriage emerge.

3. In those situations in which no coherent aboriginal culture patterns have been maintained, family patterns are built up through combinations of individuals, rather than through linkage of kin groups. The combinations most often made will be between unrelated males and females, and will be of a class here called marriage. The absence of traditional sanctions plus the new economic independence of women tend to make these unions unstable and of short duration. The demographic picture, with its imbalance in sex and age ratios, is seen as being of primary importance in creating and maintaining these patterns.

OCEANIA

Melanesia — In many parts of Melanesia wage labor has become a necessity to the present way of life of the natives. In some respects the situation resembles that in certain parts of Africa, but until after World War II little urbanization and detribalization resulted from the migrancy. Rather, the pattern of migrant labor at first became integrated into previously existing cultural patterns. One still does not encounter urban centers with the characteristics described above for Africa, although there is some evidence that this may soon develop (Spoehr 1963, various articles). Though some men who migrate do not return to their villages, it is reported that many of these nonreturning men actually marry women from other nearby tribes and go to live with their wives' kin (Hogbin 1939:162).

H. I. Hogbin, describing the situation in the Solomons just before World War II, gave the following reasons for men becoming absentee laborers: (1) to see the world, (2) to raise their social status, and (3) to get money. The money was used to buy manufactured items and, more important, to pay taxes and brideprice (*ibid.*:161). Actually, rather than paying brideprice in cash, as is now common in Africa, the men might use the money to buy customary articles (shells, beads, and the like) for presentation as brideprice.

Wages which the young men receive from work are distributed more regularly according to kinship obligations than is the case in Africa, where disposal of wages is increasingly becoming an individual matter. In the Solomons elders expect to receive a certain portion of the youths' earnings so that they too might pay taxes and buy goods. In return, the elders help the youths accumulate brideprice.

One effect of migrant wage labor sometimes reported in Melanesia is the unbalancing of the sex and age ratios in the villages, so that persons staying behind may find it difficult to maintain the native economic system. Thus, in some areas the villagers complain that the gardens suffer from lack of manpower, and that more work must be done by the older people and women to make up for the absence of the young men. Although it is true that at times in the past labor was forcibly recruited from certain islands for work on plantations and in mines, and that some areas were thus seriously denuded of manpower, this phase is long-since past; and at the same time, technological improvements have made it possible for fewer persons to maintain production (Hogbin 1958:172; Salisbury 1962).

Another result of the system has been the undermining of traditional authority patterns. Young men who go away, see the world, and return with money and tales of Western customs and ideas gain prestige. In effect, knowledge of the outside world rather than wisdom in tribal lore gains the respect of the group. The new knowledge, moreover, tends to invigorate the migrant-labor system, for it creates new material wants, which require more money. Families encourage their sons to migrate so that they may contribute to the well-being of the entire group.

This seems to have had two primary effects on marriage. First, since the young men seldom marry before going out to work, the marriage age of men is delayed. Hogbin says that most boys leave home at the age of about seventeen or eighteen, an age at which they formerly would have thought of marriage. They stay away for periods ranging from four to ten years before returning home to obtain a wife and settle down. Hogbin (1958:194) suggests that divorce in rural areas is possibly less common than in the past, and that monogamy and personal preference in mate selection have also increased, though there has been a continued respect for rules of lineage and clan exogamy.

Another factor of primary importance is that many islanders have entered into Western economy not by wage labor, but by producing and selling copra from their own lands. If the hypotheses presented here are valid, we would not expect the consanguineal household pattern to arise in such situations. C. S. Belshaw (1955:34) points out that in Ware, Southeastern Papua, copra making is the concern of individual families, and that the household consists usually of an elementary family (*ibid.*:15). This type of system appears to parallel in many ways the *poquitero* banana sales formerly carried on by the Black Carib.

More recent data for other parts of Oceania suggest that the situation has changed considerably since World War II. The most striking case for present purposes is that reported by Paul Kay, in which he describes a residential section of urban Tahiti (Papeete). He found that 46.5 per cent of the households in the section known as Manuhoc contained no complete nuclear family, and that they tended to be dominated by women among whom consanguineal relations formed the basis for common residence and cooperative ties (1963:66–71). Kay links this situation with three factors: (1) rural-to-urban migration, (2) a lack of permanence in residence even when the men reach the city, and (3) economic insecurity for males. Interestingly enough, he compares this situation with that found in the Caribbean and says, "the structural aspects of household composition — the formal similarities of these two household types, so widely separated in historical and cultural terms, are striking" (*ibid.*:70).

In the same symposium C. S. Belshaw suggests the "likelihood of the emergence (in Pacific towns) of a substantial number of families in which the mother is the stable person of orientation, as in parts of the West Indies, and in some southern African cities" (1963:19).

Although these comments are provocative, it should be emphasized that these situations may include only the matrifocal family and not the consanguineal household, as herein defined. We are told little about the role of the male as a brother-son in a consanguineal type of household. However, it seems very likely that such a situation exists in Kay's study site. If this is so, it should furnish the final blow to theories which derive this form only from the historical circumstances of slavery and African origin. Clearly, other factors are involved in the development of such forms in the Pacific area.

In summary, it appears that migrant wage labor in the Pacific has brought about distinctive social changes and that the series of marriage and household types noted for the Black Carib, although possibly now developing in some areas, does not regularly occur. Absence of these structures seems to result from the fact that traditional organization has remained relatively stable, and that previous marriage and family forms have thus persisted through changes which for the most part have failed to transform the pre-existing culture. The type of migratory pattern, which here seems to return the male to his village for later permanent settlement, would seem to be a crucial difference between the situation in the Pacific and that in the Caribbean. It is likely that this pattern is now changing and moving in the direction of recurrent migration and permanent removal, in which case we may expect further changes in family organization — perhaps in both the rural and the urban zones.

AUSTRALIA

It appears that among some aborigines wage labor long ago became important, but, as in Melanesia, the young men went away to work, then returned and settled down, the aboriginal patterns of marriage and family life being little altered. On the other hand, in urban centers there are groups of mixed-bloods who engage exclusively in wage labor. Among these people, particularly in New South Wales, there exists evidence of both the marriage types and the household forms with which I am dealing (Calley 1956; Reay 1951). Divorce is common, and many marriages are fairly casual relationships in which neither party expects or desires a permanent bond to develop. Nevertheless, such unions are not frowned upon, and the children resulting bear no social stigma. It is common to find a woman with several children fathered by different men cooperating with some adult kinsman, such as her mother, a brother, or a sister (Calley 1956:202–03). Unfortunately, there is not a great deal of information available on this situation, and it would be necessary to know more of the actual nature of the various personal interrelationships involved before categorically stating that this situation is identical to that found among the Caribs. We are not told, for example, of the type or amount of economic cooperation between various pairs of adults.

It is significant to note that these groups of mixed-bloods have been rejected by, and themselves have rejected, the aboriginal patterns of culture; yet, on the other hand, they are not accepted by the whites whom they are trying to emulate (Elkin 1949:637). They have, in short, no traditional cultural or ethnic identity, and, as such, they fall into the class I have labeled "neoteric societies." A. O. Neville reminds us that "the history of the coloureds [half-castes or mixed bloods] dates back only to the coming of the whites to Australia. They are a people without tradition, lacking culture, spiritual inheritance or guidance of their own" (1951:276). Women have opportunities for achieving economic independence, but, as in Africa, they must still cooperate with some other adult(s) in order to function effectively after they have children.

There are no figures available concerning the sex ratio in these areas, so I am unable to say whether this affects family or household composition. On the other hand, there is a normal distribution of old people in the towns, and it has been reported that women with their children often live with a parent, most usually their mother (Reay 1951:118). Neither do we have good data on the usual type of residence following marriage, but in view of the indirect evidence, it appears that this may be local, depending mostly on the man's economic circumstances.

THE UNITED STATES NEGRO

Much has been written on the Negro family in the United States, most of it by sociologists. They have not generally been prone to attribute its characteristics to African survivals. Indeed, when this idea is suggested, usually by anthropologists, the sociologists tend either to deny the possibility, or to consider it a fairly weak and irrelevant argument. Nevertheless, most writers do use a historical argument in explaining the presence and importance of the consanguineal household among certain classes of American Negroes today. Instead of referring to African cultural traditions, they attribute it to conditions during the period of slavery (Du Bois 1908:21, 37; Frazier 1931:368–87; King 1945:101; Myrdal 1944:II, 931). Some writers use functional explanations in an attempt to analyze the kinds of marriages and families existing among them. These often have to do with economics, but as yet there does not seem to be much recognition that these family and marriage types may belong to a social *system*, whose parts behave in certain ways under varying influences. The tendency has been to consider the situation from the point of view of broken homes, divorce rate, illegitimacy, and sexual immorality. Behind this seems to lie the supposition that the nuclear family based upon a system of monogamous marriage is the ideal, and that all other cases are to be considered as evidences of disorganization.

The existence among American Negroes of a household and marriage system which, though different from that found among the bulk of the United States population, is nevertheless functional for certain segments, is shown only indirectly through the case histories given by these sociologists. Its parallels in other parts of the world are similarly neglected by the majority of writers concerned with the problem among United States Negroes. After constructing a description from material presented primarily by sociologists, I shall attempt to analyze the situation from the comparative point of view, showing its similarities to other societies described herein.

The family pattern is generally discussed from the point of view of the number of "woman-headed" households present in United States society as a whole. Writers have been able to show that in both rural and urban areas of the South there is a larger proportion of households with woman heads among Negroes than among whites (Frazier 1948:103). E. F. Frazier describes a woman household head as "a woman — single, widowed, divorced, or if married her husband is not living with the family — who is regarded as head of the family" (1957b:316). I would suggest that in order to understand the system we need more information than what is here given or implied. We should examine the exact composition of such households and discover whether there is any difference in this regard between Negro and white woman-headed households.

The implications are that these households are made up of one female adult plus her children, and furthermore that these are *young* children. In addition to knowing the actual composition of the households, we need to know something of the personal interrelationships among the members and the function of each within the unit. Furthermore, it would be important to know whether there are close connections between such households and nonresident persons, or between several such households.

In the absence of any statistical information concerning the exact composition of these households, we are fortunate to have helpful case histories. The following item is illustrative:

There was, for instance, a thirty-eight-year-old woman who had left her husband after five years of marriage, because, as she said, she "got tired of staying with him" and preferred to "be with mamma and them." She was working on a "two-horse farm" with her brother, who took care of her until the settlement was made at the end of the year. That she usually received nothing at the end of the year was of no importance to her as long as she lived with her mother and brother and sister" [Frazier 1948:112].

Elsewhere in the literature are frequent references to women living with consanguineal relatives of various sorts and bringing up their children within this unit. It is noted that there is an extremely strong affective bond between mothers and children (including both daughters and sons) which lasts throughout life. There also appears to be a strong tie between brothers and sisters. As in the West Indies, uterine siblings, whether or not they have the same father, have far stronger ties to each other than children of the same father by different women. Indeed, the latter may not know each other. Even when the children reach adulthood, the consanguineal units are loath to lose either females or males. C. S. Johnson tells us that in Macon County, Georgia, young people are discouraged from marrying early, and if this does happen the couple encounters a pronounced social disapproval (1934:48). When

the children finally do marry, there is strong pressure for them
to continue living in their natal units. Thus, one finds the same
pattern of duolocality previously discussed for the Carib. Although the husband and wife may at times live together,
whether in their own home or in that of one or the other set of
parents, it appears that when they split up (and the divorce or
separation rate is high) each returns to the natal group. The
unit which maintains coherence through time is built up
around a nucleus of adults related consanguineally, not affinally. Different members may come and go for various reasons,
but affinal ties rarely form the basis for a stable family. Although it appears that women have a great deal of authority in
their homes, authors often note that the mother's brother is
present, without specifying what his authority position may be.

In regard to marriage, most writers tend to define this on
the basis of duration of the union. Common-law or consensual
marriages are sometimes mentioned, but they are rather fuzz-
ily defined, for short-term ethnic unions usually are not considered marriages by sociologists. The difficulty with this sort of
classification has been pointed out before, since it is impossible
when looking at any new union to know whether it will or will
not endure, and thus whether it is or is not a marriage. The
question of how long a union must last before it is classed as a
marriage is also an insurmountable problem with this definition of the institution. This classification often has little to do
with the way in which the union is regarded by the society,
and I believe that any definition of "marriage" must ultimately
be relativistic in that it takes into account the approval of the
society in question.

Some students of Negro society have recognized this necessity. In speaking of the Negro during the years between Emancipation and the opening of the twentieth century, Frazier
says, "A large proportion of the so-called marriages were, to
be sure, 'common-law' relationships. But from the standpoint
of stability and community recognition, these relationships had
the same character as legal marriages" (1957b:628). John-

son, in *Shadow of the Plantation* (p. 66), tells us that "Sexual unions resulting in birth of children without the legal sanctions are of several types, and cannot properly be grouped together under the single classification of 'illegitimate.'" He then goes on to point out that some women deliberately choose a man to father a child for them because they want a child but do not want either the restriction of formal marriage or the constant association of a husband. Other children are born of temporary unions for pleasure. Neither of these cases is condemned by the society, unless it is felt that a man has taken advantage of a girl. It may not be overbold to note the parallel to the situation among the Black Caribs in which any union is considered legitimate by the society so long as it is carried on in the open and is admitted by both parties, and, in the event that children result, the man admits his paternity.

It is obvious that, using these as criteria of marriage, the statistics given for numbers of "legitimate" versus "illegitimate" births for Negroes in the United States are meaningless for present purposes. Also, it is apparent that the classification I set up previously for marriages and households in Black Carib society can probably be applied with equal usefulness to certain classes among United States Negroes.

I must point out that the patterns of which I am speaking here most certainly do not apply to *all* Negroes or Negro groups in the United States. The very fact that several sets of standards exist among them indicates that factors other than the historical experience of slavery must be brought in to explain the consanguineal household pattern. Frazier has repeatedly stressed the fact that the patterns described above exist among United States Negroes in both urban and rural areas of the South, as well as in lower-class families in northern cities (1948:103; 1957b:328–29). The outstanding factor to be considered in determining social class, not only among whites, but among Negroes as well, is the economic: that is, amount and kind of income.

The Negro in the South has relatively limited opportunities

for earning a living. The later industrialization of the South meant that there were few openings for unskilled workers except in agricultural enterprises, such as plantations, lumbering, or highway construction. Most of these tended to be seasonal and were poorly paid. The alternative, if a man had no land — and most did not — was to rent a small plot, generally on the tenant or sharecropper system, and try to eke out a living in this way. This living was rarely above a subsistence level. In addition, there was a limit to the number of people who could be so supported, both in terms of the individual family on a given plot and in terms of the southern Negro population as a whole.[3]

One of the earliest solutions to the problem that Negro leaders attempted was education. It was felt that somehow higher education — generally concerned primarily with subjects such as agriculture or domestic science, or the professions of nursing, medicine, law, or teaching — would help to alleviate conditions in the South. It may have had some effect in helping some individuals to raise their standards of living, but of course it did nothing, and could do nothing, to change the system itself.

What helped most to alleviate the situation was a series of migrations out of the South. These were of two types. Of the first type, represented by several mass movements between 1879 and 1930, probably the largest was during World War I, when Negro laborers were recruited for northern industry to take the place of men gone to war and of foreign whites whose entrance to the States was prohibited (Haynes 1913:106; Johnson 1927:555; Myrdal 1944:I, 193; Woodson 1918:172). Although many of the Negroes who went north in these migrations eventually returned to the South, in general this was a permanent migration which resulted in the large Negro populations that are found today in such industrial centers as New

[3] Hortense Powdermaker, in *After Freedom*, discusses the sharecropper system thoroughly, giving statistics on amounts of land, seed, size of crop, income, and the like (1939:82–85).

York, Chicago, and Detroit. It might be added that the influx was increased by large numbers of Negroes who came from the West Indies at the same time. I shall refer to this again later.

The second type of migration occurred within the South itself, the participants remaining migratory rather than settling. Large numbers of Negroes moved from place to place, finding unskilled wage labor where they could. This labor was primarily agricultural.

One of the most important differences between these two types of migration is that the first included women, though this does not necessarily mean that men and women went as conjugal pairs to the North seeking work. It seems that the migrants were primarily single individuals. Women found work in the North in factories, and especially as domestic servants. In the South there was some movement of young women into the urban centers, where they also worked as domestic servants, but the migratory harvest hands, railroad workers, and the like were nearly all men. During the depression of the 1930's, when large numbers of people, both Negro and white, turned to migratory labor as the only way of living, it was noted that the whites traveled in family groups, all members helping in the fields, while the Negroes in the camps were almost all men. In addition, the Negroes generally informed investigators that they intended to return to their home states eventually, while the whites continued on westward to California, which they had heard offered permanent work of all kinds (Brown and Cassmore 1939:24–25). This type of migration was a new pattern for most of the whites, and essentially a different one from that of the Negroes.

The situation in the South depended upon two economic bases — the small plot of ground on which subsistence crops were grown, primarily by women and children, and migratory wage labor by the men who returned occasionally (and ultimately) to the land where they still had kinship ties.

In the urban centers of the North, although there was some

moving from city to city in response to changes in the ratio of supply to demand in labor, there was more of a tendency to settle for longer periods in one place. Wages in general were higher in the North, and though job security was rather low for the Negro, who was the first to be fired when production slumped, nevertheless he did not have to move as far or as often as his brother in the South. Some jobs — such as those of Pullman porter, janitor, cook, waiter, and "redcap" (among others) — came to be considered peculiarly "Negro," and there was little competition for them from whites. The combination of relatively higher wages and more job stability made it possible for some Negroes to marry and set up households according to the standards set for them by the whites. Eventually, with better and more accessible education, many Negroes became professionals, serving the large Negro population in the cities. From these beginnings there arose a new set of criteria upon which to ascribe status. Where formerly lighter skin color had been of prime importance, now education and wealth became the basis of prestige (Frazier 1957a:198). In spite of this, the great masses of Negroes in the North remain in the lowest economic groups and have not achieved stability in their jobs or in their family life. It is among this latter group, as well as the Negroes in the rural South, that the mother headed or consanguineal household still in some measure survives (King 1945:100).

As my observation of the Black Caribs has demonstrated, the core of such a household may be any combination of primary kin, but most often it is mother and adult child. Although it is true that the oldest woman usually is considered to be the "head," the term "mother-headed" or "woman-headed" family seems to obscure the associations without which the group could not function effectively. The natural strength of the mother-child relationship is increased by economic interdependence and by a value system which places great emphasis upon the child's obligations to his mother and to his uterine siblings, even after he reaches adulthood, and which provides greatest emotional security within this unit. Although it is necessary for men to travel away from the home in order to increase the economic security of the family, the fact that they may always return to their consanguineal kin during hard times and receive food and shelter keeps them bound more closely to this unit than to any household in which they have set up affinal relationships. In the latter units the man's primary role is to propagate children, but this is not enough to make him acceptable unless he also contributes economic support. Only when he becomes financially secure can he afford to cut ties with his consanguineal household and set up a different kind of unit based on affinity (Du Bois 1908:129; Johnson 1934:48). In any system where the majority of the men are unable to achieve job security with an adequate minimum wage, we would expect to find consanguineal cores with a series of unstable temporary relationships between the women of the household and outside men. When such men leave to work elsewhere, there is nothing to assure their continued loyalty and eventual return to this household. Therefore, new relationships or unions are constantly being made and broken.

This situation holds true in general for both rural and urban areas, even though the structures of the economic systems in each are somewhat different, as we have seen. Another factor, possibly of great importance, with which I have dealt in discussing the African and Black Carib populations, is the sex ratio. Among the total United States Negro population, women outnumber men at most ages from mid-adulthood. At birth there are more males than females, but the ratio is very low — 1,029 males per 1,000 females during the years 1915–48, compared with 1,056 for the United States whites during the same period (McMahan 1951:273). However, in 1930 the United States Negro population showed an excess of females from age thirty-six, compared with an excess from age fifty in the white population for the same year (Yerushalmy 1943:46). In every census since 1890 there has been an excess of Negro females over males in New York City and in the whole nation (Du Bois 1908:19, 36; Reed 1926:93). These figures can only hint at the situation, for it would be imperative to have figures on numbers of each sex in every decade from specific localities of the country in order to demonstrate correlations with social patterns. As early as 1908 W. E. B. Du Bois suggested that the sex ratio among Negroes was one cause for what he termed "wide sexual irregularity" (p. 18). He also recognized that the economic condition of the United States Negro affected his sex mores in two ways. First, low wages contributed to postponement of marriage until a later age; and second, differential economic demand for men and women increased the disproportion of the sexes in any given area (p. 36).

Therefore, in spite of the differences in economic structure, and regardless of whether the sex ratio is a factor, I believe that from a functional point of view the consanguineal household exists among lower-class United States Negroes as a response to their precarious position in the economic system. Malinowski, in speaking of what he termed the "disintegration of the family," said, "it is a phase which occurs in all societies under the stress of economic misery" (1945:60). A sociologist, Charles E. King, stated much the same thought when he said, "The maternal family will continue to exist as long as the economic insecurity of men exists" (1945:103).

THE CARIBBEAN

For purposes of this discussion I shall define "Caribbean" to include all the islands in the Greater and Lesser Antilles, generally known as the West Indies, as well as certain areas on the mainland of Central and South America. Although J. Gillin (1951) has emphasized the differences within the area, primarily in terms of race, language, and political division, I believe that there are enough basic similarities among the sociocultural systems in this geographical area to warrant considering it a single culture area for our purposes here. In the social realm, for example, F. Henriques (1953:104) has suggested that a single family organization occurs throughout the Caribbean. It should be noted that most, but not all, of the peoples within this area are Negro or of mixed Negro descent. Only Cuba, Puerto Rico, and Santo Domingo in all the Caribbean are not completely dominated in numbers by the Negro race (Tannenbaum 1947:7). A combination of historical and contemporary circumstances has acted to develop and maintain the culture of these groups in such a way that they differ less among themselves than does any one of them from non-Negro groups in the area, such as Indians or Mestizos of Latin culture.

Various suggestions have been made to explain why these cultural similarities exist over such a broad area and why they are found almost exclusively among Negro peoples. Some writers look primarily to historical factors, such as African provenience, borrowing from European and Indian culture (primarily Carib, but also Arawak, at least in earliest times), or the effect of the conditions imposed by the European masters during the slave period. Others tend to emphasize present-day circumstances which they feel have molded all these cultures into a similar pattern. Some have suggested a combination of two or more of the above factors. Herskovits (1946) places great emphasis upon the coming together of the African and European traditions, which produced a new pattern of culture different from either but showing unmistakable resemblances to both. Most other writers' interpretations involve blending the conditions imposed by slavery with the influences of the present-day economic patterns in the area.

The crux of the argument seems to lie in the aspect of culture with which the various workers are dealing. Phenomena of social organization do not seem susceptible to piecemeal diffusion such as is observed for items of material culture, ceremony, folklore, and beliefs. Herskovits, though he took note of the patterns involved in social structure, was far more concerned with those aspects of culture which do tend to diffuse readily.

The question, then, of whether the presence of this or that culture trait should be explained in terms of historical or functional analysis depends entirely upon what sort of trait is involved. Tracing the essentials of Haitian *vodun* to Africa is certainly justified, but likening the range of family or household patterns in the Caribbean to those in Africa has little utility and, moreover, is actually misleading. A careful analysis of household types found today in both areas shows few similarities between the two, except where the same or similar contemporary conditions can also be shown to exist. Emphasizing the African custom of polygyny, in which each wife has a separate household with her children, and likening this to the New World consanguineal household obscures the functional differences which actually exist between these two systems, in spite of their apparent structural similarities. In addition, this interpretation ignores the fact that similar household systems exist among non-Negro groups in the Caribbean area, for example, in Puerto Rico, and in certain parts of Central America (see below).

Serious objections also can be made to attempts to trace the system back to slavery. I agree that the consanguineal household existed among Negro slaves, not only in the West Indies but also in the United States. However, the ancestors of groups such as the Black Caribs apparently never went through a period of slavery, so we cannot explain by this means the fact that they too exhibit the consanguineal household pattern. I would also agree that the economic and inter-class social institutions found in the area today parallel functionally, if not structurally, those that existed when the sugar empire was at its height.[4] This type of analysis enables us to arrive at a sim-

[4] M. G. Smith (1954) has shown that "slavery" per se does not necessarily produce similar social conditions wherever it occurs. He feels that the New World Negro slave–master relationship was unique and that the conceptual orientation of the British — an inconsistent set of principles

pler explanation of the phenomenon wherever and whenever it may appear.

The consanguineal household pattern has long been recognized by workers in the West Indies, though here again it generally has been interpreted in terms of breakdown and disorganization of the nuclear family. Part of the reason for this is, as I have noted for the Black Caribs, that the nuclear family does exist as a general ideal and in actual fact among the higher socioeconomic classes. If one happens to be studying only among people in the latter groups, it may well appear that the nuclear family is the most important form both structurally and functionally. Martha W. Beckwith, one of the first modern observers to study Jamaica, claimed that the patriarchal neolocal nuclear family was the typical form (1929:54). She also mentioned the presence of concubines, but primarily from the point of view of the male, not of the concubines themselves. Beckwith was, of course, mainly interested in gathering data on folklore, and she made no intensive study of the family or social structure in general. More recently, Judith Blake (1961) has suggested that legal marriage, monogamy, and the nuclear family are indeed not only the *preferred* forms, but that stigma attaches to the unmarried woman and her illegitimate offspring. This view is generally different from that presented by other students of Caribbean social organization.

Goode has recently dealt with the impact of industrialization upon family systems in various parts of the world, including the Arabic Islam countries, sub-Saharan Africa, India, China, and Japan (1963). He argues that industrialization, through its many processes, breaks down the extended family and that the nuclear family then emerges. However, Goode is primarily concerned with changes in value orientations and *ideal* patterns of family organization. In his section on Africa — the only area covered by both his and this work — he says,

---

including racism, *laissez faire*, and Christian universalism — led to the emergence of the peculiar patterns found today in the Caribbean.

"The situation in many urban African areas is precisely like that which has been described for Caribbean countries, and for many of the countries in the New World generally. Essentially, the girl must enter a consensual union, and thus risk pregnancy, in order to get a husband" (*ibid.*:184). His view (like Blake's) is that extraresidential mating or consensual cohabitation are best interpreted as forms of promiscuity because legal marriage and the nuclear family remain sought-after and prestigious goals (*ibid.*:185).

Henriques (1951, 1953) first outlined the range of family types found in Jamaica and noted the frequency and importance of the household which included no male in the role of husband-father. He attempted a classification of family types, but, unfortunately, his criteria are mixed, and the classification confuses the concepts of marriage and the family. Thus, he included (1) the Christian family — neolocal, monogamous, the marriage bond based on legal or Christian rites; (2) faithful concubinage, which differs from (1) only in that the marriage is common law; (3) the grandmother family, which included no person bound by any sort of marriage ties, but consisted instead of a group of women and their children; and (4) the keeper family, which was different from (2) only in that the common-law marriage was of relatively short duration (1951:19; 1953:104–14).

Though I credit Henriques' insight into the nature of the situation in Jamaica, his classification is not entirely satisfactory because it is not consistent. It does, to a certain extent, suggest the nature of the interpersonal ties existing among the adult members of the family. He also relates the different types to variations in age and in size and regularity of income, which are often correlated with each other, but he suggests that the situation is ultimately referable to the slave social structure and to the "psychological atmosphere of freedom," which permeated all aspects of life after the emancipation (1951:23). It seems somewhat difficult to reconcile these two factors into a logical explanation of a form which was essentially the same before and after slavery.

Several writers have pointed out the increasing shortage of land available to the Jamaican peasant and have linked this to such things as the tremendous rate of migration, both internal and external, as well as to the fragility of the marriage tie and to family disorganization (Huggins 1953; Poole 1951; C. C. Taylor 1953). Edith Clarke, in an interesting study of land holding in Jamaica, has presented evidence which shows that the nuclear family is the most prevalent and stable in areas where the land pressure is least. On the other hand, among people who were almost entirely dependent on wage labor on a large sugar estate she found the highest rates for "unstable unions, promiscuity and irresponsible parenthood" (1953:83). However, in speaking of the family in general in all the areas she studied, Clarke says, "the kindred, the blood relatives and in particular the maternal kin, as distinct from the conjugal or household group is the most important institution in our communities and often the only vital one" (*ibid.*). Clarke's material permits partial reconstruction of the interpersonal relationships which exist in these communities. She gives many instances of cases in which the sons as well as the daughters live with their mothers in adulthood (*ibid.*:90, 94, 95, 105, 115). She stresses the fact that plots of land are inherited by "all the children," regardless of sex or birth order, though in fact a will may often favor a particular son or daughter who has remained on the land to care for the old parents until they die. In any case, the typical residential group on a given plot of land is a group of siblings, real or classificatory (that is, cousins) who have inherited the land in common from *either* their mother or their father. Spouses of this group may live on the land during their lifetime, even if they are widowed, provided they do not remarry, and in no case may their children by outside partners share in the inheritance of the land. In spite of her observation that residence on the land is not a factor of importance in determining rights of inheritance, Clarke says, "the fear of the sisters that, if they do not occupy and use the home, their brother may attempt and even succeed in establishing individual ownership, has its result in their separation from the several fathers of their children" (*ibid.*:105). Thus, she emphasizes competition for land as one factor which increases the divorce or separation rate.

Another aspect of this situation which bears on our problem is that, given this type of inheritance, which necessarily increases in each generation the number of persons entitled to use the land, there must be some way of sloughing off a certain number of possible claimants in each generation. Unilineality is one systematic way of doing this, primogeniture or ultimogeniture is another, but, as we have seen, neither of these exists in this society. Clarke does not deal adequately with this problem, though certain of her statements give us an idea of how it may be accomplished. For example, she notes that quite often a parent will favor one child over another for personal reasons, leaving all the land to that individual. When this happens, there may be grumbling and dissatisfaction among the other siblings, but they accept the will as valid. Usually in such cases, however, the other children have already left the family home area, and this merely prevents them from making claim in the future — it does not put them out of a home.

Another factor which alleviates the situation is that a given child *may* inherit rights in two areas — that of the mother and that of the father. In this case the inheritor will generally exert his rights in only one of these areas, and his children will thus not be included in the next generation of heirs to the land abandoned by this parent.

Finally, since much of the land in Jamaica which is involved in this pattern of ownership is not very productive, and since many of the plots are useless for anything other than house sites and small gardens, many young people migrate permanently to Kingston or even to areas outside of Jamaica itself. Though theoretically these children may at a future time return and claim their share of land, they may find that their siblings greatly oppose such a claim.

This is another example of a society in which are found groups of persons descended from a common ancestor acting as corporate bodies within a system in which descent is bilateral. I have already pointed out that these nonunilinear descent groups exist among the Black Caribs (Solien 1959b). The effect of such methods of reckoning descent is to produce more than one descent group in which an individual may claim membership. A variety of circumstances unique to the life history of the individual will determine with which one he ultimately cooperates. He may also move from one group to another during the course of his lifetime.

It has been noted by other writers that the land situation is so acute in Jamaica that nearly all males, as well as many females, are forced to work at wage labor at least part of the time. That this has been true for some time for many West Indian islands is shown by the figures on emigration from the islands. West Indians went in considerable numbers to Colombia, Nicaragua, Honduras, Guatemala, and Costa Rica during the period from 1885 to the early 1930's, after which restrictive immigration policies closed most of these countries to Negroes. They were employed primarily in the banana and sugar industries in those countries (M. J. Proudfoot 1950:14).

From 1884 to 1888 and again from 1905 to 1913, large numbers of West Indians worked on the Panama Canal project. Between 1900 and 1924 there was another outward movement into the United States, which was decreased considerably by restrictive immigration in 1924 (Mary Proudfoot 1953:31–18). Although we know that many of these workers remained in the area to which they migrated, the majority eventually returned to Jamaica.[5]

In addition to this migration away from the island, there has always been and still is a great deal of population movement

[5] A more recent discussion of migration from the West Indies may be found in Davison (1962).

within the country. Because of the seasonal nature of most of
the employment available in the rural agricultural areas, men
tend to move from plantation to plantation following the different crops, and then either to Kingston to find other temporary jobs, or to the family plots to fill in the slack season
(Huggins 1953; Poole 1951:86). Wages are seldom high
enough to support the men while they are away from home
and to take care of all the needs of the households which they
leave behind. Neither are they sufficient to tide them over the
gap when little employment is available (August to January).
Given such circumstances, it is highly important for most men
to be able to claim rights in some household group. Here again
it is to his consanguineal group that the man returns. He not
only has an inherited right to reside on this land, but the net-
work of kinship ties ensures his inclusion in a group of people
obligated to give him hospitality, regardless of how much cash
he may bring into the household. Thus, whether one looks at
the situation from the point of view of the men who migrate to
work, or from that of the women who stay behind, the consanguineal household is the most effective enduring social unit. It
is better able to withstand the vicissitudes that might be created by the necessary absences of the men than any type of
conjugal household. In the consanguineal household there are
usually a number of men who may fill the "brother" role. If
one of these is lost, the group is not disrupted. In the conjugal
family household, however, the permanent loss of the single
man filling the husband-father role would create serious dis-
turbances. Since one is never absolutely certain that a man will
return, it is a rare woman who can afford to detach herself
from her consanguineal group, or to depend completely on
any one man — especially since, as I have pointed out above,
the man's wages will more than likely be insufficient to support
her and the children. Although she may seek support from her
husband's family, this too is an unreliable source, since her
rights there are far more tenuous than they are in her own fam-

ily. Her *children* may claim rights in their father's area, but she is there only by virtue of the family's toleration.

It is clear from reports on other areas in the Caribbean that the consanguineal household pattern exists fairly strongly in all. Herskovits' work in Haiti and especially in Trinidad shows that the pattern exists, though his analysis does not go as far as I have attempted here. He notes the prevalence of *placage*, or concubinage relationships, and in general relates these to economic factors, pointing out that legal Christian marriage confers a great deal of prestige but is possible only for those at the upper levels of income. He also points out that many men have "two wives" between whom there is a great deal of quarreling. He suggests that the influence of Christianity has affected the "psychological set" of the people in regard to plural marriages, a customary and accepted tradition in Africa, and has interfered with the smooth functioning of the pattern in the New World (Herskovits 1937; Herskovits and Herskovits 1947).

The Black Carib culture also shows a pattern of quarreling between co-wives, but I cannot agree that Christianity as such has greatly influenced the attitudes of the people in regard to morals or ethics, either in marriage or in other aspects of culture.

An important work on this type of family or household among Caribbean Negroes is that of Raymond T. Smith in regard to British Guiana (1956). He has presented a wealth of material, both qualitative and quantitative, on frequencies and importance of the various forms within the society, and has related each form to economic circumstances. He also emphasizes that the nature of the class-color system prevents Negro males from engaging in many types of work which would secure them a better and more stable income. This situation is true for other parts of the Caribbean, and is undoubtedly best considered as a phenomenon which grew out of the peculiar relations between master and slave in the area (M. G. Smith 1954). Looking at the obverse side, the Negro man is continually being pressured into taking certain jobs which are considered to be appropriate for persons of his color. I have already indicated that this phenomenon has existed, and to a certain extent still does exist, in the United States. Negroes have long been recruited by large companies for work in the malaria-infested lowlands of Central America, since it was early recognized that they seemed to be less susceptible to this disease than were other racial groups. Out of this practice grew the rationalization that Negroes were peculiarly fitted for handling bananas, both on the plantations and on the docks in Central America and in Jamaica itself.

Although the interpretation offered here agrees essentially with Raymond Smith's work, and has been greatly aided by it, the report lacks details on the actual relationships existing between various members of the family, which makes it difficult to ascertain the nature of the consanguineal household (called "matrifocal family" by Smith). We are told only that a certain percentage of families are "woman-headed," but we learn little about how such families actually function on an interpersonal level. Because Smith has stressed the negative factor of the man's role, he is led into stating that this "matrifocal system of domestic relations and household grouping . . . can be regarded as the obverse of the marginal nature of the husband-father role" (R. T. Smith 1956:221). This may be true, but I do not believe that it has explained very much about the nature of the family itself. I also think that his cross-cultural comparisons provide exceedingly weak support for his contentions. Since we are never certain from his description just what the matrifocal family *is*, other than that it is "woman-headed," it is difficult to evaluate the comparability of the societies he has included in this section. Thus, he discusses J. Gillin's work on Moche, Peru, Oscar Lewis' Tepoztlan study, and a community study made in Scotland by a team of British anthropologists, including Shirley Wilson, who studied family organization. Apparently the only thing these three communities had in common was that there were households "headed" by women and that, to varying extents, the groups in question lived within a broader social system in which a certain amount of discrimination against the smaller group existed. As a matter of fact, in Moche the family pattern actually was that of the nuclear family, but the woman had a "dominant position," and it was presumably on this basis that Moche was included. Actually, the consanguineal household was not really typical of *any* of the groups discussed. Again, it seems that his procedure has been faulty in that he does not make it clear just how he actually defines the "matrifocal" family. In some cases it seems to mean only that the women have a great deal to say about how money is spent, while in others the woman is the primary source of income. Possible cooperative ties with other persons are mentioned here and there, but not stressed, and certainly not included in his definitions and classifications.

Since the field work upon which this study is based was done, many works presenting new data on one aspect or another of the Caribbean family and household system have appeared — most of them in unpublished form. (See, for example, Davenport 1956; Greenfield 1959; Kreiselman 1958; Otterbein 1966; M. G. Smith, 1962a; Vallee, 1964; Peter Wilson 1961; and Whitten 1965.) In addition, M. G. Smith's comparative analysis of family structure in five Caribbean communities is an important contribution (1962b). It has not been possible in this monograph to discuss each of the above, but I have so far found nothing to contradict the points being made here. Smith's work, because of the amount of data it brings together and analyzes, and because of the fact that it discusses many or most of the specific problems raised by others, deserves special comment.

In addition to his comparative work (1962b), we are especially indebted to M. G. Smith for his description of the family and household system of Carriacou, where consensual cohabitation is rigorously forbidden, but where males regularly engage in extraresidential unions in addition to legal marriages involving common residence of spouses (1962a). He is quite right in insisting that the mating system in the Caribbean may be viewed as one determining factor in the development of the various domestic or household structures described. Thus he says, "The mating system operates as a formative principle in family structure because it establishes relations between as well as within household groups, changing their composition and mediating the establishment of new units" (1962:219). However, even though we may accept this view, we are left with no adequate explanation for the different forms of marital unions themselves. Here I have treated the mating system only implicitly, believing that the various forms of union are, like household structures, themselves reflections of the different ways in which individuals are pressured by the economic system, which in turn is related to ecology, as has been well described by Clarke (1957).

Another point emphasized by Smith is that most investigators have failed to recognize the role of collateral kinship in the constitution and development of household units (1962b:218). This de-emphasis of the maternal grandmother seems unnecessary for a number of reasons. First of all, Smith's own figures do not show a significant difference, as he implies they do, between the likelihood that a child will live with its mother's mother as opposed to its maternal collateral kin. Furthermore, since the grandmother is an older person and may be expected to die earlier than a younger relative, the placement of a child with its collateral kin may be seen as merely an extension of the principle of dependence upon the mother's consanguineal kin. In short, Smith's work, although it incorporates a number of different explanatory devices, seems to support the general view taken here.

I have so far not mentioned the non-Negro or predominantly Mestizo-mulatto portions of the Caribbean. Although there is less information on family structure for areas such as Cuba and Puerto Rico than there is for other parts of the Caribbean, it is possible to search the literature for descriptions of customs and institutions suggestive of the type of system I am here describing. J. H. Steward's *The People of Puerto Rico*

(1956) has provided a wealth of information on different populations in that island. E. R. Wolf, speaking of a coffee municipality in Puerto Rico, says,

Under consensual marriage, it is possible to change marriage partners, and the children in a household sometimes come from previous marriages of both parents. Often, however, a woman keeps all of her own children when she remarries. This is especially true where the man has left the municipality in search of a job elsewhere or where he has proved to be ineffective as a provider [1956:258].

He goes on to point out that because of this situation, women form the stable part of the household, while men tend to be on the fringes of the successive households in which the women are dominant. This community, in the western highlands of Puerto Rico, is not unusual. In Nocorá, a sugar plantation, Elena Padilla Seda notes that "In the absence of property and matters of inheritance, consensual unions are extremely common, and although these may be enduring, separation is so easy that the wife, together with her progeny by any number of consorts, is the permanent core of the home" (1956:313). In the same volume S. W. Mintz describes a similar situation for Cañamelar, another sugar plantation (1956:375–78).

In spite of this information, we still cannot say with certainty whether the consanguineal household exists in these societies. *If* there were always enough men so that all women of marriageable age could depend on getting another husband when a separation occurred, then probably the consanguineal household would have no purpose. We are not told what happens to old people, or to women left alone with their children. Mintz gives us some notion of the interrelationships among men and their female kin. He notes that single men have an obligation to help their own mothers, while married men must help their wives and mothers-in-law. He believes that this suggests a tendency to structure social relationships along the female line (*ibid.*:380). In speaking of a man without a wife, he notes a villager's comment, "Poor Juan. He has no woman.

His clothes tear and stay torn unless his sister mends them . . ." (*ibid.*:378).

In view of the conditions that I have set up for the appearance of the consanguineal household, I believe it likely that this unit may be found in these Latin Caribbean societies. The studies of the area make it clear that the majority of the lower-class peoples in Puerto Rico depend upon wage labor of some sort for a living. Certain studies suggest that the labor force on the island is to an extent migratory (Crist 1948:182; Poole 1951:83; Wolf 1956:258). Many of the people who make up this labor force are descendants of the group formerly known as *agregados*. During the settling of Puerto Rico, many free whites and mulattoes sought refuge from the civil and military authorities by fleeing to the highlands. There they eked out a bare existence from the soil, using land which they claimed only as squatters. In 1824, the Spanish forced many of these people to work in the sugar plantations, since there was a dearth of slaves in the island and no more could then be purchased readily. Others remained in the highlands and became attached to coffee plantations. At the turn of the present century the coffee industry began to lose ground to the sugar industry, promoted by the United States. Many of the mountain peasants, called *jibaros*, as well as the small owners and workers of the coffee plantations, migrated to the coast looking for work. They formed a great reservoir of cheap labor. Poole reports, "Family ties are loose among these floating laborers and illegitimacy is common" (1951:83).

Such a society, having been created by the conditions to which it has adapted, would fit my definition of a "neoteric" society. The only factor which I have not been able to check is the sex ratio. I would, however, suggest the probability that the consanguineal household exists among these people of Puerto Rico.

H. L. Safa has presented information from a lower-class urban Puerto Rican community which supports this prediction, made on the basis of materials available to me in 1957.

She also agrees essentially with the reasoning of R. T. Smith and rejects the historical explanations given by others (1964:5).

One other society deserves attention before we leave the Caribbean area. Lying only on the border of the area I have outlined, it is of similar culture. This is the area studied by H. W. Hutchinson in northeastern Brazil. He describes a number of different types of families, one of which, his "Class D" family, is especially interesting here. This family type consists of a woman or women with children, various relatives, boarders, and a class of persons called *agregados*, who live in the home temporarily and who do not pay board.[6] Many of these are actually the lovers or common-law husbands of the women who are considered to be the chief members (1957:151). Hutchinson does not make it clear just who the "relatives" are, or what their relationship to the woman "heads" is, so I cannot say with certainty whether this parallels the consanguineal household. However, from the evidence he does give, it seems very likely that it does. He points out that marriage is most often consensual among this group, and that children almost always remain with the mother after a breakup. Finally, in one of the most important clues he gives, Hutchinson tells us that this type of family exists only in the urban areas where the women can find work to support themselves and their families. They may receive monetary help at various times from different men, but they seldom form stable relationships with them. In contrast, he notes that a scarcity of women in the rural plantation zone makes it easy for them to find new husbands if the old ones die or desert (*ibid.*:56).

This seems to me to suggest that the consanguineal household exists in Brazil under social and economic conditions compatible with those I have set up as being conducive to the appearance of this form.

[6] Note that this usage of the word is completely different from that found in Puerto Rico.

THE AMERICAN INDIAN

The literature concerning the acculturative patterns of the various American Indian societies nowhere points to the consanguineal household as a typical adaptive form, with the possible exception of the Pomo, as I shall show below. In spite of the tremendous differences in Indian cultures at the time of the conquest, and the variations in the circumstances involved in their conquest and acculturation, the resulting social patterns today have much in common. In part this is probably due to the fact that all these groups are living within a single political and cultural unit, the United States, and that in recent years at least all have been affected by more or less common policies and prejudices.

Most observers report "breakdown" in the institution of marriage, meaning that unions have become less stable and often are not begun by a recognized ceremony, whether legal or according to Indian custom. However, coresidence of a man and woman is everywhere the custom, and in at least one society, the Wisconsin Winnebago, is the criterion by which a union is judged proper (Lurie 1952:202; Oestreich 1948:126). There are many types of families described, but all of them appear to involve at least one conjugal pair. The nuclear family seems to be increasing in frequency among most groups.

Although wage labor is important to many Indian groups, it is generally of a nature quite different from that found in the United States among Negroes or in the Caribbean. Among the Blackfoot migrant labor is relatively unimportant, but when it does occur, usually whole families move together (Hanks 1950:57, 70). This is also true of the Winnebago (Oestrich 1948:64), certain groups of Iroquois (Randle 1951:177), and the Papago of Arizona (Joseph, Spicer, and Chesky 1949:98).

The primary source of income for most American Indian groups today seems to be production for sale of one or another commodity. In general, farming has never proved popular or profitable among most groups. Nevertheless, many groups do sell a certain amount of produce, and some groups raise cattle (Hanks 1950:58).

Another consideration in explaining the seeming absence of the consanguineal household among the American Indians today is the fact that these groups are living under the aegis of a highly developed political system. Even though most of the groups would probably have to be considered "traditional" in the typology here presented, the government which controls them has made available institutions which enable a divorced or deserted woman to support her children without finding it necessary to cooperate with some other kinsman. At least one writer has pointed out that in some instances women whose husbands cannot support them completely are better off being divorced, since they may obtain Aid to Dependent Children (Lurie 1952:203).

Although the consanguineal household does not seem to exist among American Indians, there is one apparent exception. The Aginsky's description of modern Pomo society suggests that this form might exist among them (1947; 1949). The Aginskys point out that women are fairly dominant in Pomo society and must be considered the mainstay of the family. Marriages are extremely brittle, and children invariably stay with the mother (Aginsky 1947:85; 1949:611). Although their description sounds very suggestive, nowhere do they describe the actual structure or functioning of the typical household, so it is impossible to say whether this is an example of the consanguineal household system. The Aginskys maintain that the traditional Pomo culture was completely destroyed by the Spaniards and early Americans, and that social units were broken up to provide laborers, servants, and concubines for the conquerors (1947:86). Statements made by S. F. Cook support the latter view, and he also suggests that the California missions played a part in this cultural and social upheaval (1943a:145–46; 1943b:87; 1943c:2).

Although the Aginskys do not tell us a great deal concerning the economic system of the Pomo, they do stress that the women's dominant position is enforced by their economic independence (1949:613).

Since the case for the Pomo is not conclusive, and since I have found no other evidence for the existence of the consanguineal household among American Indian groups, I conclude that it does not exist as a norm among them. The reasons for this have been suggested above, and consist partially in the economic circumstances, partially in the characteristics of the larger society within which these groups live and its relationship to them. The minimal matrifocal household, made up of a mother plus her children, appears to be the more prevalent adaptive form under these circumstances.

In summary, there is evidence to indicate that the consanguineal household exists as an alternate form among the mixed-bloods in New South Wales, Australia, among lower-class United States Negro groups, probably in urban Tahiti, and quite generally throughout the Caribbean area, including Brazil and Ecuador. It is possible that it also exists among the Pomo of California, although the evidence is inconclusive. It is very likely that the form exists in other societies not considered here, and I would suggest that it be looked for wherever the conditions here held to be conducive to its development are found.

Seven

~~~~~~

SUMMARY AND CONCLUSIONS

~~~~~~

IN the previous chapters I have described a particular form
of household grouping which I have termed the "consanguineal household." This has been defined as a coresi-
dential group of people who live under one roof, who eat and
sleep together, and cooperate daily for the common benefit of
all, and among whom there exist no conjugal pairs. Rather, all
relationships among the members are based on consanguinity.
This group is seen as a structured unit which occurs as a response to certain economic and social conditions in societies
undergoing acculturation to Western civilization.

In order to illustrate the structure and function of the consanguineal household, I have described it as it exists in one society, that of the Black Caribs of Livingston, Guatemala. For
this purpose it was necessary to place the form within its
broader cultural and social matrix, and to view it both syn-

chronically and historically. Therefore, I have described other aspects of Carib society, and have outlined the historical events which I believe contributed toward the development of the form in this particular society. I have stressed especially the relationship between the consanguineal household and the economic organization of the society.

I emphasized initially that aside from the special case of the matrilineal Nayar, the consanguineal household never exists as the *only* household form within the total social system. Rather, it is always found as one of a series of forms, all of which are unstable and may readily change from one to another. However, the consanguineal household, which nearly always contains persons bound together in a mother-child relationship, is the only type which all members of the society experience at some time or another in their lives. Most do belong to affinal households for a time, but some *never* experience this type of residence. Relatively speaking, then, the consanguineal unit is the most stable in the society as a whole.

The nucleus of the consanguineal household in terms of composition is usually a mother and a child. This dyad may often reside alone in the more complex societies that include institutions designed to take over some of the functions of the family or household. This is the situation so often found among low-income groups in the United States, where federal assistance, in the form of Aid to Dependent Children, is available only when no husband-father figure is attached to the household. Among the Black Caribs, this unit can live in isolation only when the children are old enough to require little care and can themselves take over some of the daily domestic tasks, or when the woman is furnished a cash income large enough to free her entirely from any sort of remunerative occupation, thus enabling her to devote full time to housekeeping. However, even in the latter case, the labor involved in keeping house in this society is such that a woman with several small children is almost impossibly burdened unless she cooperates with other adults in certain domestic activities. Thus, even though approximately one-half of the *consanguineal* households in Livingston at the time of the study consisted of one woman plus children, the institution of the residential compound described above furnished a group of kinsmen upon whom such women could depend for assistance. In some such cases the custom of "borrowing" older children, who help out with the housekeeping tasks in return for their support, was a solution.

Black Carib society shows that the consanguineal household may give way to the affinal (especially nuclear family) household only when the social and economic conditions in the larger, external, or Western world offer to the males an opportunity to secure an adequate, stable, wage income. As shown in the preceding chapters, this occurs in Carib society only when a man becomes a white-collar worker or skilled laborer. This usually, though not always, involves leaving his home village and territory and seeking a place in a more cosmopolitan area, such as Guatemala City, Belize, Tegucigalpa, or some city in the United States. On the other hand, merely working and living in a city does not automatically mean that affinal families may exist and function effectively. If economic security remains precarious, the consanguineal unit remains strong. An affinal household may become consanguineal at any time if the husband-father loses economic security.

High frequencies of "common-law marriage," divorce, and "illegitimacy" seem to accompany the consanguineal system. However, these *may* exist in a society which does not include the consanguineal household as a norm. Therefore, although these increased frequencies may often serve as signposts in spotting such systems, their presence alone is insufficient evidence for assuming the existence of this type of household.

In an attempt to delineate characteristics of the society as a whole which operate to maintain the consanguineal system through time, I have suggested three factors, all of which seem to be necessary for the appearance and continuance of this system:

1. Migrant wage labor.
2. A "neoteric" quality to the society.
3. An imbalance in the sex ratio, resulting in an excess of adult females over males.[1]

I have shown that all three of these factors exist in Carib society, but in order to test their general validity, I have investigated the literature and made some cross-cultural comparisons. The societies were chosen for comparison according to two criteria: (1) those whose description included a household form which appeared to be consanguineal as I have defined it, and (2) those characterized by the presence of one or more of the three factors listed above. I then attempted to show whether or not each society fitted my typology, and if not, why not. At times I have referred to specific, interacting groups of people known by a particular name and sharing a common culture. At other times I have taken larger groups, or even generalized to a whole area which included peoples of various cultures who belonged to many distinct societies. It must be remembered that the type of society in which we would expect to find the consanguineal system is one which has recently been formed or crystallized, and in many instances its members do not feel any ethnic linkage among themselves. That is, they have no name for themselves, no distinct traditions, dress, or customs. In a sense, they are now identifiable as a "type" rather than as members of a particular sociocultural system. Actually the Carib, although they still form an ethnically distinct society in the rural areas, are increasingly becoming immersed in a larger Central American urban proletariat which includes non-Carib Negroes and Mestizos, all of whom have been subjected to similar recent influences. Although I have not specifically studied these latter groups, observations made

[1] Number 3 here may be seen as merely a corollary of Number 1, for migrant labor generally produces this effect.

during the field work suggest to me the strong possibility that the consanguineal household exists among them as well. For some purposes, then, we could ignore the cultural differences that exist between Carib and non-Carib groups of the Atlantic coast of Central America, and view them together as a "type" of society.

It seems probable, in the world of today, that most neoteric societies will be found in urban areas of the developing countries where migrants from many places increasingly settle down and break the ties with their traditional cultures and communities. Yet even then the development of the consanguineal household will probably depend in part upon the sex ratio. When women become more numerous in towns and cities — in part because of increased employment available to them there — we may expect to find patterns such as those described here, so long as the job situation for men remains precarious.

The Black Carib rural situation may prove to have counterparts only in the Caribbean, since neoteric societies have rarely formed in the countryside except under the unique circumstances of slavery in the New World. Further research, however, may disclose other cases.

It seems clear that the consanguineal household with a mother-child dyad at its core cannot be viewed as the product of any one historical tradition. It is found in widely separated areas of the world, and it appears to be related to the process by which traditional societies become adapted to the modern industrial world and lose their characteristic configurations in so doing. The fact that the less-than-nuclear family and household is neither the ideal nor the statistical norm anywhere is probably at least partially related to the difficulties a single woman has in maintaining such a unit in the developing societies. She must have outside assistance, and whether it is provided by a series of husband figures or by her kinfolk will depend upon the relative availability of persons in each of these categories. Even though a permanent monogamous marital union is the most desirable solution in all of the societies reviewed, it seems well recognized that this situation can be achieved by only a few. This problem is in turn directly related to the employment opportunities available to the men.

That the matrifocal family and the consanguineal household are so strikingly prevalent in the Americas among descendants of Africans may be explained by the fact that neoteric societies formed here sooner than elsewhere because of the disruptions brought about by the slave trade. Although sometimes interpreted as evidence of social disorganization, the consanguineal household form can also be viewed as a mechanism by which such societies manage to adapt themselves to changing conditions and survive in spite of the hardships imposed upon them by the larger system. Thus, this form serves as an adaptive mechanism for both the individual and for the society affected. As individuals become acculturated and manage to find niches for themselves in the economic system of the larger society, they tend to abandon the way of life and ideology described here. As has been repeatedly reported, legal marriage and the nuclear family are often symbols of middle-class status. Similarly, from the point of view of the society as a whole, as the industrial system becomes better established and raises the economic security and standard of living, the consanguineal household may eventually disappear. However, this is not to say that society, like individuals, will necessarily become increasingly characterized by legal marriage and the nuclear family. The course of evolution may well lead to still different forms, each adapted to the conditions of the future.

BIBLIOGRAPHY

ABBREVIATIONS

AA American Anthropologist
SES Social and Economic Studies
SWJA Southwestern Journal of Anthropology

ADAMS, R. N.
　1956　*Encuestra sobre la Cultura de los Ladinos de Guatemala.* Guatemala.
　1960　"An Inquiry into the Nature of the Family." In *Essays in the Science of Culture,* ed. Gertrude E. Dole and Robert L. Carneiro. New York. Pp. 30–49.
AGINSKY, B. W. AND E. G.
　1947　"A Resultant of Intercultural Relations." *Social Forces* 26:84–87.
　1949　"The Process of Change in Family Types: A Case Study." *AA* 51:611–14.
BANKS, E. P.
　1956　"A Carib Village in Dominica." *SES* 5:74–86.

143

BARD, S. A.
    1855   *Waikna: Adventures on the Mosquito Shore*. New
            York.
BARNES, J. A.
    1951   *Marriage in a Changing Society*. Rhodes Livingston
            Papers, No. 20. New York.
BASCOM, W. R.
    1941   "Acculturation among the Gullah Negroes." *AA*
            43:43–50.
BECKWITH, MARTHA W.
    1929   *Black Roadways*. Chapel Hill, N.C.
BEFU, HARUMI
    1963   "Classification of Unilineal-Bilateral Societies."
            SWJA 19(4):333–55.
BELSHAW, C. S.
    1955   *In Search of Wealth*. American Anthropological As-
            sociation Memoir, No. 80.
    1963   "Pacific Island Towns and the Theory of Growth."
            In *Pacific Port Towns and Cities, a Symposium*, ed.
            Alexander Spoehr. Honolulu. Pp. 17–24.
BLAKE, JUDITH
    1961   *Family Structure in Jamaica*. New York.
BLEHR, OTTO
    1963   Action Groups in a Society with Bilateral Kinship:
            A Case Study from the Faroe Islands." *Ethnology*
            2(3):269–75.
BRIGHAM, W. T.
    1887   *Guatemala, the Land of the Quetzal*. New York.
BROWN, M., AND O. CASSMORE
    1939   *Migratory Cotton Pickers in Arizona*. Washington,
            D.C.
BURDON, J. A. (ed.)
    1931   Archives Brit. Honduras, Vol. I. London.
    1934   Archives Brit. Honduras, Vol. II. London.
    1935   Archives Brit. Honduras, Vol. III. London.
CALLEY, M.
    1956   "Economic Life of Mixed-Blood Communities in
            Northern New South Wales." *Oceania* 26:200–213.

CAMPBELL, A. A.
1943   *St. Thomas Negroes — A Study of Personality and Culture.* Psychological Monogr. No. 55(5).

CLARKE, EDITH
1953   "Land Tenure and the Family in Four Selected Communities in Jamaica." *SES* 1:81–118.
1957   *My Mother Who Fathered Me.* London.

COHEN, Y. A.
1954   "The Social Organization of a Selected Community in Jamaica." *SES* 2:104–34.

COOK, S. F.
1943a   *The Conflict Between the California Indian and White Civilization. I. The Indian Versus the Spanish Mission.* Ibero-Americana, No. 21.
1943b   *The Conflict Between the California Indian and White Civilization. III. The American Invasion, 1848–1870.* Ibero-Americana, No. 23.
1943c   *The Conflict Between the California Indian and White Civilization. IV. Trends in Marriage and Divorce since 1850.* Ibero-Americana, No. 24.

CRIST, R. E.
1948   "Sugar Cane and Coffee in Puerto Rico." *Amer. Jour. Econ. and Socio.* 7:173–84, 321–37, 469–74.

CUMPER, G. E.
1954   "A Modern Jamaican Sugar Estate." *SES* 3:119–60.

DAVENPORT, WILLIAM
1956   "A Comparative Study of Two Jamaican Fishing Communities." Ph.D. dissertation, Yale University.
1959   "Nonunilinear Descent and Descent Groups." *AA* 61(4):557–72.

DAVISON, R. B.
1962   *West Indian Migrants: Social and Economic Facts of Migration from the West Indies.* London.

DU BOIS, W. E. B.
1908   *The Negro American Family.* Atlanta Univ. Publ., No. 13.

EDWARDS, B.
1818–19 *The History, Civil and Commercial, of the British Colonies in the West Indies.* 5th ed. 4 vols. London.

146 *Bibliography*

ELKIN, A. P.
1949 "Position and Problems of Aborginal Mixed-Bloods in Australia." *Proc. Pac. Sci. Congress* 7:629–37.

EVANS, DAVID K.
1966 "The People of French Harbour: A Study of Conflict and Change on Roatan Island." Ph.D. dissertation, University of California, Berkeley.

FORTES, M.
1949 "Time and Social Structure: An Ashanti Case Study." In *Social Structure: Studies Presented to A. R. Radcliffe-Brown*, ed. Meyer Fortes. Oxford. Pp. 54–84.

FRAZIER, E. F.
1931 "Family Disorganization Among Negroes." *Opportunity* 9:204–7.
1942 "The Negro Family in Bahia, Brazil." *Amer. Socio. Rev.* 7:465–78.
1948 *The Negro Family in the United States.* Rev. ed. New York.
1957a *Black Bourgeoisie.* Glencoe, Ill.
1957b *The Negro in the United States.* Rev. ed. New York.

FREEMAN, J. D.
1961 "On the Concept of the Kindred." *J. Royal Anthro. Inst.* 91(2):192–220.

FRIED, JACOB
1959 "Acculturation and Mental Health Among Migrants in Peru." In *Culture and Mental Health*, ed. Marvin Opler. New York.

GILLIN, J.
1951 "Is There a Modern Caribbean Culture?" In *The Caribbean at Mid-Century*, ed. A. C. Wilgus. Gainesville, Fla. Pp. 129–35.

GONZALEZ, NANCIE L. SOLIEN
1961 "Family Organization in Five Types of Migratory Wage Labor." *AA* 63(6):1264–80.
1965 "The Consanguineal Household and Matrifocality." *AA* 67(6):1541–49.

GOODE, WILLIAM J.
1964 *The Family.* Englewood Cliffs, N.J.

GOODENOUGH, W. H.
1955   "A Problem in Malayo-Polynesian Social Organization." *AA* 57:71–83.
1962   "Kindred and Hamlet in Lakalai, New Guinea." *Ethnology* 1(1):5–12.

GOODY, J. (ed.)
1958   *The Developmental Cycle in Domestic Groups.* London.

GOUGH, E. K.
1952   "A Comparison of Incest Prohibitions and the Rules of Exogamy in Three Matrilineal Groups of the Malabar Coast." *International Archives of Ethnography* 46(1):82–105.

GREENFIELD, SIDNEY M.
1959   "Family Organization in Barbados." Ph.D. dissertation, Columbia University.

HAMMEL, EUGENE A.
1964   "Some Characteristics of Rural Village and Urban Slum Populations on the Coast of Peru." *SWJA* 20(4):346–58.

HANKS, L. M. and JANE
1950   *Tribe under Trust, a Study of the Blackfoot Reserve of Alberta.* Toronto.

HAYNES, G. E.
1913   "Conditions among Negroes in Cities." *Annals of the Amer. Acad. of Poli. Sci.* 49:105–19.

HENRIQUES, F.
1951   "West Indian Family Organization." *Caribbean Quarterly* 2:16–24.
1953   *Family and Colour in Jamaica.* London.

HERSKOVITS, M. J.
1937   *Life in a Haitian Valley.* New York.
1941   *The Myth of the Negro Past.* New York.
1943   "The Negro in Bahia, Brazil: A Problem in Method." *Amer. Socio. Rev.* 8:394–402.
1946   "Problem, Method, and Theory of Afro-American Studies." *Phylon* 7:337–54.
1952   "Some Psychological Implications of Afro-American

148   Bibliography

Studies." *Proc. Internat. Congr. Americanists*
29:152–60.

HERSKOVITS, M. J. and F. S.
1947   *Trinidad Village*. New York.

HOGBIN, H. I.
1939   *Experiments in Civilization*. London.
1958   *Social Change*. London.

HOUDAILLE, J.
1954   "Negroes Franceses en América Central a fines del
siglo XVIII." *Antropología e Historia de Guatemala*
6:65–67.

HUGGINS, H. D.
1953   "Seasonal Variation and Employment in Jamaica."
SES 1:85–115.

HUNTER, MONICA
1936   *Reaction to Conquest*. Oxford.

HUTCHINSON, H. W.
1957   *Village and Plantation Life in Northeastern Brazil*.
Seattle.

JOFFE, NATALIE P.
1940   "The Fox of Iowa." In *Acculturation in Seven American Indian Tribes*, ed. Ralph Linton. New York.
Pp. 259–332.

JOHNSON, C. S.
1927   "The American Migrant: The Negro." *Proc. Nat.
Conf. of Social Work*. Pp. 554–58.
1934   *Shadow of the Plantation*. Chicago.

JONES, C. L.
1931   *Caribbean Background and Prospects*. New York.

JOSEPH, A., R. B. SPICER, and J. CHESKY
1949   *The Desert People: A Study of the Papago Indians
of Arizona*. Chicago.

KAY, PAUL
1963a   "Aspects of Social Structure in a Tahitian Urban
Neighborhood." *J. of the Polynesian Society*
72:325–71.
1963b   "Urbanization in the Tahitian Household." In *Pacific
Port Towns and Cities, a Symposium*, ed. Alexander
Spoehr. Honolulu. Pp. 63–74.

KEPNER, C. D.
    1936   *Social Aspects of the Banana Industry.* New York.
KEPNER, C. D., and J. H. SOOTHILL
    1935   *The Banana Empire.* New York.
KING, C. E.
    1945   "The Negro Maternal Family: A Product of an
            Economic and a Culture System." *Social Forces*
            24:100–104.
KREISELMAN, MARIAM J.
    1958   "The Caribbean Family: A Case Study in Mar-
            tinique." Ph.D. dissertation, Columbia University.
KUNSTADTER, PETER
    1963   "A Survey of the Consanguine or Matrifocal
            Family." *AA* 65:56–66.
LAYRISSE, MIGUEL
    1957   "The Diego Blood Factor in Negroid Populations."
            Nature 179:478–79.
LEWIS, OSCAR
    1961   *The Children of Sanchez.* New York.
LURIE, NANCY O.
    1952   "The Winnebago Indians: A Study in Cultural
            Change." Ph.D. dissertation, Northwestern Uni-
            versity.
McMAHAN, C. A.
    1951   "An Empirical Test of Three Hypotheses Concerning
            the Human Sex Ratio at Birth in the United States,
            1915–48." *Milbank Memorial Fund Quarterly.* Pp.
            273–93.
MALINOWSKI, B.
    1945   *The Dynamics of Culture Change.* New Haven.
MANGIN, WILLIAM
    1959   "The Role of Regional Associations in the Adapta-
            tion of Rural Populations in Peru." *Sociologus* 9:21–
            36.
MAUDSLEY, ANNE C. and A. P.
    1899   *A Glimpse at Guatemala.* London.
MENCHER, JOAN P.
    1962   "Changing Familial Roles Among South Malabar
            Nayars." *SWJA* 18(3):230–45.

MINTZ, S. W.
    1951   "The Role of Forced Labor in Nineteenth Century
            Puerto Rico." *Caribbean Historical Rev.* 2:134–41.
    1956   "Cañamelar: The Sub-culture of a Rural Sugar
            Plantation Proletariat." In *The People of Puerto
            Rico*, ed. Julian H. Steward. Urbana, Ill. Pp. 314–
            417.
MITCHELL, J. C.
    1956   "Urbanization, Detribalization and Stabilization in
            Southern Africa: A Problem of Definition and Meas-
            urement." In *Social Implications of Industrialization
            and Urbanization in Africa South of the Sahara*.
            UNESCO. Paris. Pp. 693–710.
MUNROE, ROBERT L., RUTH H. MUNROE, and
JOHN W. M. WHITING
    1965   "Structure and Sentiment: Evidence from Recent
            Studies of the Couvade." Paper presented to the
            64th Annual Meeting of the Amer. Anthro. Assoc.
            Denver.
MURDOCK, GEORGE P.
    1960   "Cognatic Forms of Social Organization." In *Social
            Structure in Southeast Asia*, ed. G. P. Murdock.
            Viking Fund Publications in Anthropology No.
            29:1–14.
MYRDAL, G.
    1944   *An American Dilemma*. 2 vols. New York.
NEVILLE, A. O.
    1951   "The Half-Caste in Australia." *Mankind* 4(7):274–
            90.
OESTREICH, NANCY
    1948   "Trends of Change in Patterns of Child Care and
            Training Among the Wisconsin Winnebago." *Wis-
            consin Archeologist* 29:39–139.
OLIVIER, S. H.
    1936   *Jamaica the Blessed Land*. London.
OTTERBEIN, KEITH F.
    1965   "Caribbean Family Organization: A Comparative
            Analysis." *AA* 67:66–79.

1966   *The Andros Islanders: A Study of Family Organization in the Bahamas.* Lawrence, Kan.

PADILLA SEDA, ELENA
1956   "Nocorá: Workers on a Government-Owned Sugar Plantation." In *The People of Puerto Rico,* ed. Julian H. Steward. Urbana, Ill. Pp. 265–313.

PAUW, B. A.
1963   *Xhosa in Town: Studies of the Bantu-speaking Population, Cape Province, No. 3.* Cape Town.

PEHRSON, ROBERT N.
1954   "Bilateral Kin Groupings as a Structural Type." *J. of East Asiatic Studies* 3:199–202.

PHILLIPS, A. (ed.)
1953   *Survey of African Marriage and Family Life.* Oxford.

POOLE, B. L.
1951   *The Caribbean Commission. Background of Cooperation in the West Indies.* Columbus, S.C.

PORTER, W. S.
1904   *Cabbages and Kings.* New York.

POSPISIL, LEOPOLD, and WILLIAM LAUGHLIN
1963   "Kinship Terminology and Kindred among the Nunamiut Eskimo." *Ethnology* 2(2):180–89.

POWDERMAKER, HORTENSE
1939   *After Freedom.* New York.

PRICE, RICHARD
1966   "Caribbean Fishing and Fishermen: A Historical Sketch." *AA* 68(6):1363–83.

PROUDFOOT, M. J.
1950   *Population Movements in the Caribbean.* Port-of-Spain, Trinidad.

PROUDFOOT, MARY
1953   *Britain and the United States in the Caribbean.* New York.

RADCLIFFE-BROWN, A. R.
1950   *Introduction to African Systems of Kinship and Marriage,* ed. A. R. Radcliffe-Brown and Daryll Forde. London.

RANDLE, M. C.
1951   "Iroquois Women, Then and Now." In "Symposium

on Local Diversity in Iroquois Culture." *Bull. Bur. Amer. Ethnol.*, No. 149:167–80.

READ, MARGARET
1942 "Migrant Labour and Its Effects on Tribal Life." *Internat. Labor Rev.* 45:605–31.

REAY, MARIE
1951 "Mixed-Blood Marriage in Northwestern New South Wales. A Survey of the Marital Conditions of 264 Aboriginal and Mixed-Blood Women." *Oceania* 22:116–29.

REED, RUTH
1926 *Negro Illegitimacy in New York City.* New York.

RIVERS, W. H. R. (ed.)
1922 *Essays on the Depopulation of Melanesia.* Cambridge.

ROBERTS, G. W.
1957 *The Population of Jamaica.* Cambridge.

SAFA, H. L.
1964 "From Shanty Town to Public Housing: A Comparison of Family Structure in Two Urban Neighborhoods in Puerto Rico." *Caribbean Studies* 4:3–12.

SAHLINS, M. D.
1958 *Social Stratification in Polynesia.* Seattle.

SALISBURY, R. F.
1962 *From Stone to Steel, Economic Consequences of a Technological Change in New Guinea.* New York.

SCHAPERA, I.
1947 *Migrant Labour and Tribal Life.* London.

SCHEFFLER, H. W.
1966 "Ancestor Worship in Anthropology: Or Observations on Descent and Descent Groups." *Current Anthropology* 7(5):541–51.

SIMPSON, G. E.
1952 "Discussion of Paper by Jean Price-Mars." *Proc. Internat. Congr. Americanists* 29:148–51.

SMITH, M. G.
1954 "Slavery and Emancipation in Two Societies." *SES* 3:239–90.
1962a *Kinship and Community in Carriacou.* New Haven.
1962b *West Indian Family Structure.* Seattle.

SMITH, R. T.
1956   *The Negro Family in British Guiana*. London.
SOFER, C.
1956a   "Urban African Social Structure and Working Group
        Behavior at Jinja, Uganda." In *Social Implications of
        Industrialization and Urbanization in Africa South
        of the Sahara*. UNESCO. Paris. Pp. 693–710.
1956b   "Adaptation Problems of Africans in an Early
        Phase of Industrialization at Jinja, Uganda." In
        *Social Implications of Industrialization and Urbani-
        zation in Africa South of the Sahara*. UNESCO.
        Paris. Pp. 613–23.
SOLIEN, NANCIE L.
1959a   "The Consanguineal Household Among the Black
        Carib of Central America." Ph.D. dissertation, Uni-
        versity of Michigan.
1959b   "The Nonunilineal Descent Group in the Caribbean
        and Central America." *AA* 61:578–83.
1959c   "West Indian Characteristics of the Black Carib."
        SWJA 15:300–307.
1960   "Family and Household in the Caribbean." *SES*
        9(1):101–6.
SPOEHR, ALEXANDER
1963   *Pacific Port Towns and Cities, A Symposium*.
        Honolulu.
STEWARD, J. H. (ed.)
1956   *The People of Puerto Rico*. Urbana, Ill.
TANNENBAUM, F.
1947   *Slave and Citizen, the Negro in the Americas*. New
        York.
TAYLOR, C. C.
1953   "Some Land Situations and Problems in Carib-
        bean Countries." In *The Caribbean: Contemporary
        Trends*, ed. A. C. Wilgus. Gainesville, Fla. Pp. 59–73.
TAYLOR, D. M.
1938   "The Caribs of Dominica." *Papers of the Bureau of
        American Ethnology* 3:109–59.
1951   *The Black Carib of British Honduras*. New York.

TEJADA V., CARLOS, NANCIE L. S. DE GONZALEZ, and
MARGARITA SANCHEZ
   1965   "El Factor Diego y el géne de Células falciformes
          entre los Caribes de raza negra de Livingston,
          Guatemala." *Revista del Colegio Médico de Guate-
          mala*, 16(2):83–86.
THOMPSON, LAURA
   1940   *Fijian Frontier*. San Francisco.
UNESCO (ed.)
   1956   *Social Implications of Industrialization and Urbani-
          zation in Africa South of the Sahara*. Geneva.
VALLEE, LIONEL
   1964   "The Negro Family of St. Thomas: A Study of Role
          Differentiation." Ph.D. dissertation, Cornell Uni-
          versity.
VALLEJO, A. R.
   1893   *Primer anuario estadístico correspondiente al año
          de 1889*. Tegucigalpa.
WESTERMANN, D.
   1949   *The African Today and Tomorrow*. Oxford.
WILSON, G.
   1941   *An Essay on the Economics of Detribalization in
          Northern Rhodesia*. Rhodes-Livingston Paper, No. 6.
WILSON, PETER
   1961   "The Social Structure of Providencia Isla, Colum-
          bia." Ph.D. dissertation, Yale University.
WHITTEN, NORMAN E., JR.
   1965   *Class, Kinship, and Power in an Ecuadorian Town:
          The Negroes of San Lorenzo*. Stanford, Calif.
WILLEY, GORDON R., and PHILIP PHILLIPS
   1958   *Method and Theory in American Archaeology*.
          Chicago.
WOLF, E. R.
   1956   "San José: Subcultures of a Traditional Coffee
          Municipality." In *The People of Puerto Rico*, ed.
          J. H. Steward. Urbana, Ill. Pp. 171–264.
WOODSON, C. G.
   1918   *A Century of Negro Migration*. Washington, D.C.

WOOFTER, T. J.
    1930   *Black Yeomanry*. New York.
YERUSHALMY, J.
    1943   "The Age-Sex Composition of the Population Resulting from Natality and Mortality Conditions." *Milbank Memorial Fund Quarterly*. Pp. 37–63.
YOUNG, M., and P. WILLMOTT
    1957   *Family and Kinship in East London*. London.
YOUNG, T.
    1847   *Narrative of a Residence on the Mosquito Shore*. London.

INDEX